ADRIAN HENRI
A CRITICAL READING

ADRIAN HENRI

A Critical Reading

ANDREW TAYLOR

Greenwich Exchange
London

Grateful thanks to Catherine Marcangeli and the Adrian Henri Estate and to Rory Waterman, without whom this book would not have come to fruition.

Thanks also to the staff at The University of Liverpool Special Collections and Archives for their help during visits to the Liverpool Poets archive, Racheal Eymond, James Hodgson, Professor Robert Sheppard and Professor Geoff Ward.

Greenwich Exchange, London

First published in Great Britain in 2019
All rights reserved

Adrian Henri: A Critical Reading
© Andrew Taylor, 2019

Adrian Henri poems © The Adrian Henri Estate
and Catherine Marcangeli

Printed and bound by imprintdigital.com
Cover design by December Publications
Tel: 07951511275

Greenwich Exchange Website: www.greenex.co.uk

Cataloguing in Publication Data is available
from the British Library

ISBN: 978-1-910996-28-7

This book is dedicated to the memory of
Adrian Henri, Nichola Taylor, Rachel Smith
and to my parents, E.M. and W.J. Taylor

If Liverpool did not exist, it would have to be invented
– Felicien de Myrbach

CONTENTS

INTRODUCTION

Toward the Sixties,
Liverpool and *The Mersey Sound*

Men and cities grow and learn to love
one another.[1]

Liverpool has always been about the future.[2]

LIVERPOOL IS A CONTRADICTORY CITY. ITS inhabitants, whether native or not, tend towards a fierce loyalty to the place, whereas outsiders often have a less optimistic view of the city.[3] Charles Landry argues that 'in Liverpool, people appreciate[d] the character of the place, its creativity and rebelliousness'.[4] Paul McCartney notes that Liverpool's uniqueness is in part down to the accent of its people:

> Liverpool has its own identity. It's even got its own accent within about a ten-mile radius. Once you go outside that ten miles it's 'deep Lancashire, lad'. I think you do feel that apartness, growing up there.[5]

Liverpool is also a city of myths: the city's emblem, the Liver Bird is a mythical creature said to have been based on the cormorant.[6] Determining the etymology of Liverpool is equally difficult. As with all place-name studies, historical records offer the best insights to origin. David Cottrell points to a theory that the name stems from the Old English 'lifrig' meaning 'thick with water', and a differing opinion from Victorian Liverpool architect and historian, Sir J.A. Picton who argued that the 'word has its true origin in the Welsh Llivr – "Confluence" – and Pwll – "Pool" – so that the whole word means, "the expanse at the pool" or "the pool at the confluence."'[7] A.D. Mills similarly refers to 'pool', citing the first spellings as: Lpool and Liuerpul, the latter dated circa 1190, meaning 'pool or creek with thick or muddy water'.[8]

Liverpool had long been an appealing destination for working-class people, both indigenous and from overseas, due to the port and the prospects of work. For example, the city has a large Chinese community. The first Chinese settlers came in 1834, after arriving on a ship alongside a cargo of tea. The ship had a six-month turnaround and its company J. Bibby & Co established a regular route to China in 1868, leading to a settled Chinese community in the city.[9] During the Irish potato famine in the 1840s, 300,000 people used Liverpool as an escape route. 80,000 remained in the city giving rise to a large Irish community that dispersed throughout the city and the North-West of England.[10] Such influxes brought attendant difficulties of housing stock shortages and health issues.

Liverpool was granted city status in 1880 and in 1881 it had a population of 553,000.[11] In 1886, a major exhibition took place called the 'International Exhibition of Navigation, Commerce and Industry in Liverpool, England' and Liverpool's reputation was highlighted in an 1886 edition of the *Illustrated London News*:

> Liverpool, thanks to modern science and commercial enterprise, to the spirit and intelligence of the townsmen, and to the administration of the Mersey Docks and Harbour Board, has become a wonder of the world.

It is the New York of Europe, a world-city rather than merely British provincial'.[12]

During the 1930s, massive investment took place in public infrastructure in and around the city. Examples include the Queensway road tunnel under the River Mersey, at the time the longest road tunnel in the world; the East Lancashire Road, linking the city with Manchester; and continued investment in the dock system. Work continued on the city's Anglican Cathedral. Despite an economic downturn nationwide, Liverpool took its image seriously, thinking of itself as 'the second city of the Empire', and a local text produced for schoolchildren, argued for Liverpool's 'adaptability in the face of adversity.'[13]

The Second World War inflicted serious damage to Liverpool. The city was key to the war effort, as it was a major gateway to the north Atlantic. Its port and dock system were seriously damaged during the Blitz of May 1941. In the space of a week, 2,315 bombs were dropped on the city, alongside other devices, killing 4,000 people in the area and displacing up to 70,000.[14]

The latter half of the 20th century brought many of the problems associated with post-war economic downturns, and resulted in a somewhat revitalized city. Many commentators argue that Liverpool was then placed back on the international map by The Beatles,[15] the phenomenal success of this band, started 'little less than a cultural revolution', following the release of their debut LP, *Please Please Me* in 1963.[16] However, there had been a heightened sense of creativity in parts of the city prior to the 1960s and as Adrian Henri later said, 'Liverpool in the 1950s seemed like Paris in the 1920s.'[17] The Beatles' influence is not in doubt, but in 1965 Allen Ginsberg visited the city largely because of the strong body of poets in the city, of course which included Henri. During his stay, Ginsberg delivered his memorable quote that 'Liverpool [is] at the precise moment the centre of the consciousness of the human universe.'[18]

Henri dedicated one of his most famous poems, 'Mrs Albion, You've Got a Lovely Daughter', to Ginsberg, after a visit to St George's church in Everton. St George's is located in Albion Street, which Ginsberg saw as a Blakean sign.[19]

The visit to Liverpool by Ginsberg in 1965 needs assessment, not only for the impact it had on Adrian Henri, but for the wider implications it had on the city. Ginsberg arrived in the city to be met by the poet Brian Patten. For the first few days, the American stayed in Patten's flat in Canning Street, L8, and later with Henri in his roomier accommodation on the same road.[20] During the six days in Liverpool, Ginsberg held a reading at Wilson's Bookshop in Renshaw Street, visited the art galleries, the Cavern, and the School of Art.[21] There has been much made of Ginsberg's 'Centre of the Consciousness of the Human Universe' comment, so much so that in 2007 an exhibition at Tate Liverpool adapted the quote and titled an exhibition: 'Centre of the Creative Universe: Liverpool and the Avant-Garde', and the exhibition catalogue also has a chapter devoted to Ginsberg's visit to the city with a detailed discussion of his words.[22] Christoph Grunenberg and Robert Knifton, editors of the catalogue, argue that Liverpool had at the time of Ginsberg's visit, 'achieved such a prominent status in the popular imagination, it enabled Ginsberg to make his comment emphatically.[23]

There is no doubt that the media focus on Liverpool in 1965 was overwhelmingly due to the success of The Beatles and the attendant status was largely due to this success both in the UK and America. Ginsberg's decision to come to the city was not completely independent of The Beatles, as he had been introduced to the band through Bob Dylan in London. However, Brian Patten had published Ginsberg in his small magazine, *Underdog*, alongside other American writers such as Robert Creeley, so Ginsberg would have been aware of a poetry scene existing in the city at that time. Brian Patten notes that it was Creeley who visited Liverpool first and told Ginsberg that the city had 'a great buzz.'[24]

But what contributed to Ginsberg saying this? Phil Bowen argues that 'Henri and others knew he [Ginsberg] was talking about The Beatles', and the impact that they had globally.[25] Others point to Ginsberg's character itself. Jonah Raskin notes:

> Ginsberg was in the habit of making grandiose and global statements and wanted to sound like a sage and an oracle, all at the same time. The Beatles did put Liverpool on the map of the world for most Americans – even hip Americans.[26]

However, Edward Lucie-Smith, editor of the influential *The Liverpool Scene* anthology that published Henri, Patten and McGough alongside others who were intermittently part of the Liverpool poetry scene, such as Spike Hawkins, Pete Brown and Henry Graham, associates Henri and the other poets equally, as primary influences:

> The rise of The Beatles, and the sense that Adrian Henri and the other Liverpool poets represented a commitment to Modernist, internationalist values missing from the poetry being written at that time. [...] You've got to remember that Adrian was interested in popular culture, including rock, but also very much interested in the whole early Modernist culture represented not only by the Cubist Picasso, but also by Apollinaire, the Dada writers in Zurich and so on.[27]

The book that would launch the reputations and careers of three Liverpool poets, *The Mersey Sound* (London: Penguin, 1967), continues to sell past its 50th year. Adrian Henri was joined in the anthology by fellow poets Brian Patten and Roger McGough. Much has been made of the continuing influence of the book, as typified by the *Guardian*'s description of the book as 'required reading for anyone interested in British culture', or former Poet Laureate, Carol Ann Duffy's, claim that 'the best thing that made poetry less Oxbridge was the Liverpool poets'.[28]

Brian Patten was born in Liverpool in 1946, settling in the Liverpool 8 area of the city in 1963, where he had earlier started publishing *Underdog*.[29] Roger McGough was born in Litherland, north of the city of Liverpool in 1937 and after studying at the University of Hull, he moved back to the city in 1963, living with future wife Thelma Monaghan in the Princes Park area of the city.

The three poets came together by meeting at various poetry events in the city during 1961. McGough had previously met Adrian Henri, and knew him a little. The readings took place in coffee bars such as Streate's, O'Connor's Tavern, Sampson and Barlow's, various pubs and clubs and perhaps most famously, Hope Hall, a forerunner of the Everyman Theatre, on Hope Street. Adrian Henri recalled the early readings in *Punch* magazine in 1986 saying of the readings at Sampson and Barlow's, that:

> right from the start we'd hit on an 'anyone-can-join-in' set-up [...] Some would read poems, sing, or take part in sketches McGough and others had written. Many were regular contributors, and we knew almost everyone there by name.[30]

It is important to establish the locality of these venues within the city of Liverpool. The venues were in easy reach of Liverpool 8, the area of the city (within walking distance of the city centre) where in the early 1960s, the three *Mersey Sound* poets all lived. The poets moved away from the strict parameters of the jazz and poetry mix, established at Streate's. Streate's was a coffee bar located in May Street, off Mount Pleasant, nearer to the city centre. Sampson and Barlow's was a restaurant on London Road, with a room upstairs. In the early 1960s it played host to a club called The Casanova and The Beatles played an early show there on 9 February 1961.[31] O'Connor's Tavern, was closer still to the Liverpool 8 area. On the corner of Hardman Street and Roscoe Street, in the shadow of Liverpool Cathedral, the venue was another room above a pub.

Central to the three poets becoming aware of each other and their practice, was Henri's organisation of the first 'Happenings' in the UK. Henri described the 'Happenings' thus:

> The happenings were presented as part of a Merseyside Arts Festival in 1962 and 1963, along with poetry-and-music and folk-evenings. The 'events', as we called them, quickly became a popular form of entertainment: a mixture of poetry, rock'n'roll and assemblage. The early ones like City (1962), by Adrian Henri/John Gorman/Roger McGough, used a taped music track. Later events had live music by local 'Merseybeat' groups, for instance the Roadrunners and the Clayton Squares, as in Nightblues, 1963.[32]

Henri took his cue from American artist, Allan Kaprow. Kaprow was instrumental in Henri devising the first 'Happenings' in Liverpool. Writing in *Total Art*, Henri points to the influence of Claes Oldenburg and Andy Warhol alongside Kaprow and that 'Kaprow's radical rethinking of the whole artist/audience/environment/information relationship has been a source of inspiration to many younger artists working in apparently different fields.'[33]

An insight into the early poetry readings comes from Henri himself. In an article titled 'The Poet, the Audience and Non-communication' published in *Sphinx* magazine in 1964, Henri had this to say about the audience at these early readings:

> The predominantly teenage, non-intellectual, non-student audience like to laugh with McGough and cry with Patten about the problems we all share.[34]

Catherine Marcangeli, French art historian and executor of the Henri estate, argues that the Happenings and readings were in some ways similar. Dating the beginning of the Happenings to 1962, Marcangeli notes that 'collaborations between poets, musicians and artists were already commonplace.'[35] The Happenings organized by Henri 'turned into an environment in which to juxtapose moments, situations, fragments of the everyday, images, words, music, movements, actions and interactions with an audience.'[36] The first, titled 'City', took place in August 1962 at Hope Hall.[37]

With regards to the role of poetry in the Happening, in an introduction to *City Event* (second version) which took place at Manchester College of Art in December 1962, Henri (the introduction was also signed by McGough), notes that:

> The poetry is not concerned with narrative but is rather an attempt to project emotional 'herd' atmosphere through impressionistic tactile imagery adapted from the King-size polythenescape of which we in the city are all a part (ie audiotactilism).[38]

In terms of the relationship between the audience and performer during the Happenings, Henri, writing in *Solem* magazine in 1964, issued a statement alongside a text called 'Daffodil Story: An Experiment in Communication'. He points to his poem 'I Want to Paint' and notes:

> 'I Want to Paint' is a semi-serious statement of my position on the relationship of art to environment and the mass media. A sort of manifesto in fact, which I sometimes improvise on when reading in public. [...] The experiments 'events' – are a sort of mixture of painting, poetry, music, sounds, smells, words, etc, creating a total environment which is carrying the technique of college [sic] to its logical conclusion. [...] a TV ad, my paintings, *The Waste Land*, a Michelangelo Pieta and a Beatles record are all basically involved in the same business – communication.[39]

In the extract from 'Daffodil Story: An Experiment in Communication' cited in *Solem*, we can see the collaborative elements with McGough and Patten:

5   Patten reads poem. Adrian paints huge Daffodil. 'Along Came Jones' for 2 minutes.

8   All lights out except one red. McGough and Patten read sad love poems to Blues accompaniment. Death Girl hooded, black masked, gives out dead Flowers to audience.

9   Lights on. Daffodil-Girl on bike gives out *live* flowers to audience. Adrian's 'Lakeland Poems' on tape, and Adrian paints huge flower.[40]

Writing in his autobiography, *Said and Done*, published in 2005, Roger McGough recalls his first meeting with Brian Patten, who was then a journalist on the *Bootle Times*. Patten noted that 'the modern poets are reciting poetry to PAINTING.'[41] This clearly is a response to the readings and Happenings that Henri had been central to. McGough recalls that the Merseyside Arts Festival took place in August 1962. To keep the idea of the festival in the minds of the Liverpool public, McGough, along with John Gorman, the festival organiser, decided to host a weekly series of events in the city. Henri was also active at these events which took place at Hope Hall. In a 1996 feature in the *Independent* Patten clearly recalls the first meeting of the three,

About four days after we met [McGough and Patten] at Streate's, [2 November 1961] we did a poetry-reading together with Adrian Henri in a place called Hope Hall – now the Everyman Theatre in Liverpool. We kept meeting from that point on, as part of a group.[42]

McGough points to a review in the *Manchester Guardian* of December 1962, of a Happening that was organised by Henri in Manchester, during his time in the city as a tutor at the Manchester College of Art. The event took place at the Whitworth Gallery in the city's Openshaw area. The review is useful in its descriptions of these early Happenings:

> In a room hung with advertising posters, among the bus tickets, the mangled prams and step ladders there was poetry, spoken by Mr McGough, a Liverpool teacher in corduroy jacket and jeans, the first five minutes of which were intentionally inaudible beneath the tape-recorded jazz. The spotlight fixed on a girl in a black sweat-suit, immobile beneath the step ladder. [...] The girl got up and did a snaky dance.[43]

McGough recalls that the crescendo of the piece was 'Adrian [who] threw paint all over us. It was truly ground breaking.'[44]

This is reminiscent of Yoko Ono's later performance at Liverpool's Bluecoat Arts Centre, titled 'Music of the Mind', which took place on 26 September 1967. Henri, rather tellingly, was present in the audience. Photographed taking part in a piece called 'Bandaging Yoko Ono', part of a wider piece called 'Bandaged', it seemed appropriate that Henri, as the instigator of Happenings in the UK, should be active in the piece. The *Guardian* enigmatically described the evening as 'that kind of evening' and noted the difference between the Liverpool and London audiences:

> In London, they look very intently for every last meaning in Miss Ono's performance. Here, they sang 'Daisy, Daisy show us a leg', and 'Andy Pandy's Come to Play'. Adrian Henri's pear shaped figure headed the queue to start the do-it-yourself painting. [45]

What this highlights is the differing perspectives and reactions to the readings, events and Happenings taking part in the city. The humour that the three poets were later derided for, was perhaps due to a focus on audience enjoyment over individual gratification. Henri, ever the experimentalist (McGough terms him 'Dadaesque' in some of the readings at Sampson and Barlow's) would perform his 'Silent Poems' consisting of a series of empty picture frames.

McGough would go on to describe these kinds of experimentation, as a way of breaking down the division between the audience and performer.[46]

Henri would transfer this experimentation to his selection for *The Mersey Sound* in 1967 and his debut collection from 1968, *Tonight at Noon*. If we look at a selection from the first edition of *The Mersey Sound*, 'Pictures from an Exhibition', subtitled 'Painting and Sculpture of a Decade 54-64 Tate Gallery London April-June 1964', we can see this playful experimentation:

> No 84 Mark Rothko 'Reds – No 22' 1957
> SCARLET
> ORANGE
> **ORANGE**
> ORANGE
> SCARLET
> **CRIMSON**
> SCARLET[47]

Perhaps more indicative of the work that was being produced for both the Sampson and Barlow readings and the Happenings, is 'Poems Without Words' from *Tonight at Noon*.[48] Here we can see the participatory roles of the audience:

> *POTATO CRISP POEM*
> Crisps distributed (during interval for instance) to audience, who are told not to eat them. A. then announces poem, and eats packet of crisps as noisily and quickly as possible, accompanied by audience.[49]

and from later in the sequence:

> *LOVE POEM III*
> A. holds up plastic lily-of-the-valley (Variant: Spring love poem: plastic daffodil)[50]

It is worth reproducing the entire contents of 'Summer Poems Without Words' alongside its instruction, to ascertain the flavour of the performative elements of these early readings:

SUMMER POEMS WITHOUT WORDS
(To be distributed in leaflet form to the audience. Each poem should be tried within the next seven days.)

1 Try to imagine your next hangover.
2 Travel on the Woodside ferry with your eyes closed. Travel back with them open.
3 Look for a black cat. Stroke it. This will either be lucky or unlucky.
4 Find a plastic flower. Hold it up to the light.
5 Next time you see someone mowing a lawn smell the smell of freshly cut grass.
6 Watch *Coronation Street*. Listen to the 'B' side of the latest Dusty Springfield record.
7 Sit in a city square in the sunlight. Remember the first time you made love.
8 Look at every poster you pass next time you're on a bus.
9 Open the *News of the World* at page 3. Read between the lines.
10 The next time you clean your teeth, *think* about what you're doing.[51]

Here we can see some soon to be familiar Henri themes. The black cat would appear in poetry and paintings, noticeably 'The Entry of Christ Into Liverpool'; plastic flowers, and the themes of love and travel, all appear in Henri's work throughout his career. Locale, in the form of the Woodside ferry, which is a destination at Birkenhead on the Wirral 'over the water' from Liverpool, would have been familiar to those who were handed the list at readings.

This study of Henri's work will focus solely, and largely on his poetry intended not primarily for children. There is plenty of material about his artwork in extant.[52] Exhibitions have taken place recently in Liverpool and London.[53] Henri was also a keen writer of children's poetry. Often this overlapped with publishing his poetry for adults. The final chapter, 'Legacy' will take into consideration this work. The chapters form a chronological approach to the poetry. Henri was very much an autobiographical poet. That is obvious to most readers. One only has to look at 1971's collection *Autobiography*. The journey through the poetry will reveal a poet who is vastly underrated, often reductively labelled as a 'Liverpool' poet or perhaps even more confusingly, as a 'Merseybeat' poet. As we shall see, he was also more than this.

As the celebrations for the fiftieth anniversary of *The Mersey Sound* took place between April and July 2017 in Liverpool, the city re-embraced the work of Henri, McGough and Patten.[54] 1967 was an important year for Liverpool. The Metropolitan Cathedral of Christ the King was consecrated, The Beatles released *Sgt Pepper's Lonely Heart's Club Band* and *The Mersey Sound* was published by Penguin. The city's cultural standing was second to none, for a city of its size. Part of this stems from the historical perspective outlined above, the city as a port, as a destination: often transitory and often as a place of refuge. And, of course, the influence of the popular cultural revolution, in large, caused by The Beatles cannot be underestimated. In June 1967, the band starred in the first live global broadcast. That year, they premiered a new song, 'All You Need Is Love', which was written as an anti-war anthem. The final chapter, 'Legacy' will also consider these anniversary celebrations.

Notes

[1]Charles Bukowski, 'as you slow down the mermaids look the other way', in *Slouching Toward Nirvana* (New York: Ecco/Harper Collins, 2005), p241.

[2]Paul Morley, 'Liverpool Surreal' in Christoph Grunenberg and Robert Knifton, eds, *Centre of the Creative Universe: Liverpool and the Avant-Garde* (Liverpool: Liverpool University Press, 2007), p42.

[3]The positivity generated by the announcement of the city's award of European Capital of Culture was dented by a negative story published in *The Spectator* entitled 'Bigley's Fate', dated 16 Oct 2004, regarding the capture and subsequent beheading of Ken Bigley, the Liverpool engineer working in Iraq. The magazine issued an apology after the then editor, Boris Johnson, referred to the city's 'mawkish over-sentimentality'. 'Bigley's Fate' in *The Spectator* 16 October 2004 <https://www.spectator.co.uk/2004/10/bigleys-fate/> accessed 17 April 2007.

[4]Charles Landry, *The Creative City* (London: Earthscan, 2000), p43.

[5]Paul McCartney, in Paul Du Noyer, *Liverpool: Wondrous Place* (London: Virgin Books, 2002), p7.

[6]For further material about the Liver Bird and its association with Liverpool, see David Cottrell, *The Little Book of Liver Birds* (Derby: Breedon Books Publishing, 2006).

[7]David Cottrell, *The Little Book of Liver Birds*, p15.

[8]A.D. Mills, *A Dictionary of British Place-names* (Oxford: Oxford University Press, 2003). *Oxford Reference Online*. Oxford University Press. Edge Hill University. 17 April 2007 <http://0-www.oxfordreference.com.library.edgehill.ac.uk:80/views/ENTRY.html?subview=Main&entry=t40.e8595>

[9]Information accessed at Chinatown Online, 23 April 2007 <http://www.chinatown-online.co.uk/pages/guide/liverpool/history.html>

[10]For a thorough examination of the history of the Irish in Liverpool, refer to 'Ribbonism, nationalism and the Irish pub' in John Belcham,

Merseypride: Essays in Liverpool Exceptionalism (Liverpool: Liverpool University Press, 2006), pp67-100.

[11]Table 1.1 'Population of Liverpool and Merseyside; Manchester; and Glasgow, 1801-1981' in John Belcham, *Merseypride: Essays in Liverpool Exceptionalism*, p4.

[12]David Cottrell, *The Little Book of Liver Birds*, p18.

[13]John Belcham, *Merseypride: Essays in Liverpool Exceptionalism*, p27.

[14]Information gathered on-line at Liverpool John Moores University, History on-line Project. 18 April 2007 <http://www.lmu.livjm.ac.uk/lhol/>

[15]A useful timeline from 1946 to the present day by Darren Pih and Robert Knifton appears in Grunenberg and Knifton, eds, *Centre of the Creative Universe: Liverpool and the Avant-Garde*, pp238-248.

[16]Simon Warner in Grunenberg and Knifton , eds, *Centre of the Creative Universe: Liverpool and the Avant-Garde*, p96.

[17]Adrian Henri in Paul Du Noyer, *Liverpool: Wondrous Place*, p94.

[18]The quote appeared on the back cover of Edward Lucie-Smith, *The Liverpool Scene* (New York: Doubleday & Co, 1968). To whom Ginsberg said the line is debatable but Simon Warner argues that it was said to Henri during Ginsberg's Liverpool visit. For more on Ginsberg's visit, see Simon Warner, 'Raising the Consciousness? Re-visiting Allen Ginsberg's Liverpool Trip in 1965' in Grunenberg and Knifton, eds, *Centre of the Creative Universe: Liverpool and the Avant-Garde*, pp96-108.

[19]Interview with Adrian Henri, by David Bateman in Stephen Wade, ed, *Gladsongs and Gatherings: Poetry and its social context in Liverpool since the 1960s* (Liverpool: Liverpool University Press, 2001), p90.

[20]Simon Warner, 'Raising the Consciousness? Re-visiting Allen Ginsberg's Liverpool Trip in 1965' in Grunenberg and Knifton, eds, *Centre of the Creative Universe: Liverpool and the Avant-Garde*, p100.

[21]Patten recalls the reading at Wilson's Bookshop as being 'at the bottom of Hardman Street' in personal communication with Simon Warner,

'Raising the Consciousness? Re-visiting Allen Ginsberg's Liverpool Trip in 1965' in Grunenberg and Knifton, eds, *Centre of the Creative Universe: Liverpool and the Avant-Garde*, p100; however Wilson's Bookshop until its closure in the early to mid-1990s, was on Renshaw Street at the corner with Heathfield Street. However, Phil Bowen says that the reading was in Parry's Bookshop in Hardman Street next to the Philharmonic Pub; Bowen, *A Gallery to Play To: The Story of the Mersey Poets* (Exeter: Stride, 1999), p63.

[22]The exhibition at Tate Liverpool ran from 20 February-9 September 2007. The chapter regarding Ginsberg's Liverpool visit is by Simon Warner, 'Raising the Consciousness?' in Grunenberg and Knifton, eds, *Centre of the Creative Universe: Liverpool and the Avant-Garde*, pp96-108.

[23]Christoph Grunenberg and Robert Knifton, 'The Crater of the Volcano' in Grunenberg and Knifton, eds, *Centre of the Creative Universe: Liverpool and the Avant-Garde*, p24. The Liverpool author and playwright Willy Russell offered this description of Ginsberg's quote: 'Ginsberg was only telling Liverpudlians what Liverpudlians already already knew anyway.' TV broadcast, 'The Mersey Sound: The South Bank Show', first broadcast in the UK on ITV1, 7 October 2007, directed by Bob Bee, edited and presented by Melvyn Bragg.

[24]Brian Patten in Simon Warner, 'Raising the Consciousness?' in Grunenberg and Knifton, eds, *Centre of the Creative Universe: Liverpool and the Avant-Garde*, p100.

[25]Phil Bowen, *A Gallery to Play To: The Story of the Mersey Poets*, p64.

[26]Jonah Raskin, in Simon Warner, 'Raising the Consciousness?' in Grunenberg and Knifton, eds, *Centre of the Creative Universe: Liverpool and the Avant-Garde*, p106.

[27]Edward Lucie-Smith, in Simon Warner, 'Raising the Consciousness?' in Grunenberg and Knifton, eds, *Centre of the Creative Universe: Liverpool and the Avant-Garde*, p108.

[28]Both quotations appear on the rear cover of the Penguin Modern Classics edition of the book, *The Mersey Sound* (London: Penguin Classics, 2007).

[29]For more about this area of the city and the impact it had on the Liverpool poets, see Chapter one.

[30]Adrian Henri, 'Pub Poet' in *Punch* Magazine, 15 October 1986, p12.

[31]For more about this Beatles performance, which was their first filmed show, see *The Liverpool Echo* dated 28 May 2015 <http://www.liverpoolecho.co.uk/whats-on/places-remember-city-centre-venues-9341165> This article also contains a link to the film of the band's concert.

[32]Adrian Henri, *Total Art: Environments, Happenings and Performance* (New York: Praeger, 1974), p117.

[33]Ibid, p98.

[34]Catherine Marcangeli, 'From Collage to Happening: A Feel of Reality' in *Adrian Henri: Total Artist* (London: Occasional Papers, 2014), pp124-149. *Sphinx* was a magazine that came out of The University of Liverpool.

[35]Marcangeli, p141.

[36]Marcangeli, p141.

[37]For more on this and other Henri-led Happenings, see Marcangeli, pp142-145.

[38]Catherine Marcangeli, *Adrian Henri: Total Artist*, p22.

[39]Adrian Henri, 'Daffodil Story: An Experiment in Communication' in *Solem* in Grunenberg and Knifton, eds, *Centre of the Creative Universe: Liverpool and the Avant-Garde*, p120-121.

[40]Adrian Henri, 'Daffodil Story: An Experiment in Communication' in *Solem* in Grunenberg and Knifton, eds, *Centre of the Creative Universe: Liverpool and the Avant-Garde*, p120-121. NB. 'Along Came Jones' is a recording by The Coasters.

[41]Roger McGough, *Said and Done* (London: Century, 2005), p130.

[42]Brian Patten, 'How We Met: Roger McGough and Brian Patten' in the *Independent*, Saturday 31 August 1996. <http://

www.independent.co.uk/arts-entertainment/how-we-met-roger-mcgough-and-brian-patten-1361357.html> accessed 10 April 2010.

[43] Ibid.

[44] Ibid.

[45] Michael McNay, *From the archive, 27 September 1967: Yoko Ono in Liverpool – review* in the *Guardian* 27 September 2014. <www.theguardian.com/culture/2014/sep/27/yoko-ono-bluecoats-liverpool> accessed 1 October 2014.

[46] Roger McGough, *Said and Done*, p135.

[47] Adrian Henri, 'Pictures from an Exhibition', in *The Mersey Sound*, p35

[48] Adrian Henri, *Tonight at Noon* (London: Rapp and Whiting, 1968), pp28-31.

[49] Ibid, p28.

[50] Ibid.

[51] 'Summer Poems without Words' in *Tonight at Noon*, p31.

[52] See the bibliography for such details. Aside from a few brief mentions, little attention in this book is paid to Henri's musical output as a member of 'The Liverpool Scene'. A career spanning overview of the band was released as a double CD and on vinyl, entitled 'The Amazing Adventures of The Liverpool Scene', with full liner notes. On a personal note, I met Adrian Henri only once. I visited the private view of an exhibition that he curated called 'The Dr Duncan Art Show' at the Museum of Liverpool Life, in 1997, and I was a guest of the artist Clement McAleer whose work appeared in the show. I remember Henri being warm and generous with his time, even at such a busy event. We discussed his contribution to the exhibition, the painting 'Dr Duncan in Seel Street'.

[53] Henri's work was shown as part of the Tonight at Noon fiftieth anniversary celebrations of *The Mersey Sound* at Liverpool's St George's Hall. The exhibition was titled 'Adrian Henri: Poet/Painter/ Performer'. A companion exhibition, 'The Mersey Sound Archives', took place at Liverpool's Central Library. The exhibitions took place

from 12 April-15 July 2017. 'The Mersey Sound Archives' exhibition re-titled 'The Mersey Sound at 50' transferred to The Poetry Library at London's Southbank Centre, and ran from 28 July-24 September 2017.

[54]A series of events were curated by Catherine Marcangeli for the anniversary celebrations. An exhibition of Henri's art took place at St George's Hall in the city centre, titled 'Tonight at Noon'; an exhibition of archive material from the Adrian Henri Estate and the Liverpool Poets Archive at the University of Liverpool took place at Liverpool Central Library, and a concert by former Sonic Youth founder, Thurston Moore, took place at St George's Hall Concert Room. See https://www.cultureliverpool.co.uk/tonightatnoon/ for more information.

1

EARLY YEARS AND EARLY POEMS

The Mersey Sound (1967), *Tonight at Noon*
& Other Poems (1968) and *City* (1969)

ADRIAN HENRI LIVED AND WORKED AS a poet and painter
in Liverpool for most of his adult life, settling in the city after
university in 1956.[55] He was born in Birkenhead, across the river
Mersey from Liverpool and died in the city in December 2000.
Clearly a poet of Liverpool, Henri it has been argued, 'creates a
Liverpool that is both ordinary and magical, everyday and
legendary.'[56] Of major interest, is the process that enabled Henri to
create this vision of Liverpool. In an interview with David Bateman
in February 2000, Henri said this of his early work:

> And when I began, it was like, very very pastiche T.S. Eliot, because
> I fell under the spell of Eliot completely when I was in the sixth
> form. And I wrote long, turgid, mock-Eliot sort of things: a cross
> between T.S. Eliot and teenage angst, really. And then I went on
> doing that for about ten years, I suppose, and just keeping them
> and not doing anything.[57]

This is important, as it highlights that Henri's modernist
inheritance began early in his writing career. Henri's influences
though, were wide-ranging. In an interview conducted with

Catherine Marcangeli, Adrian Henri's partner and literary executor, she highlighted the influence of Eliot alongside Charles Baudelaire and Allen Ginsberg, and noted that 'in a way the Beats and the Surrealists ran almost parallel in terms of influence.'[58] There is also an early clue to the Situationists' influence on Henri. His 1968 collection, *City*, has as its cover design an A-Z map of the Liverpool 8 area with the title blocked onto the streets in red.[59] This is arguably a conscious reference to Debord's theory of the *dérive*, as the lettering is linked and represents the routes around the streets that Henri would have walked daily.[60]

As noted in the introduction, Henri lived and worked in the Liverpool 8 area of the city during a time when the world's attention was focused upon Liverpool.[61] Darren Pih argues that 'it was after the Beaulieu Jazz Festival of 1960 that the seeds of the Liverpool 8 scene were sown.'[62] Establishments like Streate's Coffee Bar at number 51 Mount Pleasant in the city centre were holding regular poetry and jazz nights. Streate's, alongside Sampson and Barlow's, a restaurant in London Road, in the basement where Henri gave his first poetry reading, were central to the establishment of Liverpool's poetry scene in the 1960s.[63] Despite these venues being in the city centre, Liverpool 8 (later christened Toxteth, after a nearby area, by the national media during and after the 1981 riots in the city), played an important role in the city's bourgeoning bohemian culture. The geographical perspective of the area needs assessment. Liverpool 8 was named after its postcode, though there is some dispute about its boundaries. Darren Pih argues that 'there emerged a mythologised bohemian quarter whose reputation led to marked improvements in external perceptions of the city.'[64] These external perceptions led to publications such as the *Weekend Telegraph Magazine* (the associated magazine to the *Daily Telegraph*) featuring the area in an article titled 'The Sound of L8' in the edition dated 31 March 1967.[65] Pih further points to the difficulties of locating Liverpool 8 by noting that:

> Some sites regarded as being a part of Liverpool 8 bohemia in the 1960s were outside of the L8 postal district. A number of key locations, such as Liverpool College of Art and Gambier Terrace are in L1. Streate's Coffee Bar was in L3. However, conceptually and mentally these places were central to the bohemian scene.[66]

Perhaps it is best left to Adrian Henri to describe Liverpool 8 of the late 1960s by looking at his poem 'Liverpool 8', first published in Edward Lucie-Smith's anthology *The Liverpool Scene* in 1968. The following is the first stanza:

> Liverpool 8 ... A district of beautiful, fading, decaying Georgian terrace houses ... Doric columns supporting peeling entablatures, dirty windows out of Vitruvious concealing families of happy Jamaicans, sullen out-of-work Irishmen, poets, queers, thieves, painters, university students, lovers ... [67]

Today the area is much changed. The Georgian terraces remain, though rather gentrified. The Liverpool 8 that Henri refers to in his poem highlights the area's multi-racial residents and the unemployed, many who now have moved out of the area away from the Georgian terraces. The housing consisting of flats in the large terraced houses offered affordable accommodation for those mentioned in Henri's 'Liverpool 8'. The students that Henri mentions are important, as many of the students (and their teachers) lived in the nearby terraces and attended the Liverpool College of Art on Hope Street, where Henri lectured from 1964 until 1968.[68]

The College of Art was an essential ingredient to the bohemian atmosphere of the area. Ex-students of the college included John Lennon and Stuart Sutcliffe who shared a flat on nearby Gambier Terrace, behind the Anglican Cathedral. Liverpool painter, Sam

Walsh, also lived in Gambier Terrace. Walsh was a colleague of Henri's at the Art School, who sometimes took part in Henri's readings, playing guitar in accompaniment, and was instrumental in the setting up of those first poetry readings in Liverpool, as he introduced Henri to Johnny Byrne, who was one of the instigators of the city's readings.[69] This highlights the diverse mix of artists, painters and musicians who attended the College of Art.[70] Close to the college of Art on Rice Street is the pub Ye Cracke. This pub, alongside the Philharmonic pub on Hope Street, was another crucial component to the bohemian atmosphere of Liverpool 8. Its regular crowd included students, artists, and tutors such as Arthur Ballard, from the Art School and actors from the Playhouse theatre.[71] Brian Patten recalls drinking in both Ye Cracke and the Philharmonic with Allen Ginsberg when Ginsberg visited Liverpool in 1965.[72]

Unlike Roger McGough and Brian Patten, Henri used all of the poetry from his contribution to *The Mersey Sound* in his debut collection, *Tonight at Noon*. If we take a Henri poem first published in *The Mersey Sound*, 'Liverpool Poems', we can see the diverse cultural references that he employed in these early poems: a curious mix of high and low culture and references, both literary and artistic. Henri himself, in an introduction to his own work in 'Liverpool Accents: Seven Poets and a City', acknowledges the curious blend of cultural references that appeared in both his poems and his art:

> The city, and Liverpool specifically, became a locus where not only are favourite places shared with lovers mythologised, but events from any part of a cultural spectrum could be sited: [...] Alfred Jarry's monstrous Père Ubu is spotted repeatedly in the city centre.[73]

The poem comprises twelve short vignettes. Each is numbered and some contain instructive comments; we can trace this back to the Situationists with their intent of altering the perspective of the everyday, alongside the poetry performed during the Henri organised Happenings. For example, the first reads in its entirety:

> 1
> GO TO WORK ON A BRAQUE![74]

This is a clever play on the advertising slogan of 'Go to work on an egg!', which appeared in newspapers and on television in the 1960s and 1970s in the UK. It also refers to the shape of a brick in contrast to the shape of an egg, providing a suitably surreal image. Immediately, we are given a clue to Henri's fine art background with the reference to Georges Braque, a French artist (b 1882, d 1963) who, alongside Pablo Picasso in 1909, developed Cubism. In 1912, Picasso and Braque incorporated the use of collage and cubes in their work.[75] Henri had used this collage technique in paintings from the mid-1950s, while he was an art student in Newcastle. His tutor, Richard Hamilton had encouraged his students to experiment with collage.[76] Examples of Henri's collages include, '24 Collages, No. 6. Mulligatawny Soup Painting (Homage to Andy Warhol)' and 'Big Liverpool 8 Painting'.[77]

The second poem contextualises the year of the poem's composition, 1967:

> 2
> Youths disguised as stockbrokers
> Sitting on the grass eating the Sacred Mushroom[78]

The 'Sacred Mushroom' refers to the hallucinogenic family of mushrooms, Strophariaceae, commonly known as 'magic mushrooms'. Henri defamiliarizes the image by placing youths as stockbrokers, away from the traditional City locale of the dealing room, sitting on grass (perhaps a pun on marijuana) taking hallucinogenic drugs and resting while partaking in a dérivé.

In poem 4, we can again see the influence of the Situationists. The poem is Marxist in tone, surreal in outlook and shows evidence of Henri's sympathies for Anarchists:

4
PRAYER FROM A PAINTER TO ALL CAPITALISTS:
   Open your wallets and repeat after me
     'HELP YOURSELF!'[79]

The surrealist tone is highlighted in the introduction to the instructive section of the poem, linking prayer with capitalism along with the image of capitalists following the instructions of a painter active in the re-distribution of income.

Linking to the first poem, with the cultural reference of the advertising slogan, the fifth poem mentions (highlighted as if in an advertisement) a soap product. This poem also refers back to the religious reference of prayer in the fourth poem, with the phrase 'rise again on the 3rd day' relating to Christ's resurrection, and hints at a two day stay in bed:

5
There's one way of being sure of keeping fresh
LIFEBOUY helps you rise again on the 3rd day
after smelling something that smelt like other people's socks[80]

Again, one of the poems is a signifier of its time of composition. Number 6 makes reference to the British Licensing Laws of the 1960s, when public houses opened from noon until 15.45 and from 18.30 until 21.30. The laws became more relaxed, and eventually serving hours increased until 23.00.[81]

6
Note for a definition of optimism:
A man trying the door of Yates Wine Lodge
At quarter past four in the afternoon.[82]

Another reference to a higher cultural awareness appears in poem 7:

> 7
> I have seen Père UBU walking across Lime St
> And Alfred Jarry cycling down Elliot Street[83]

Jarry was a forerunner of the Theatre of the Absurd and created Ubu, a character which appears in many of Henri's paintings and poems.[84] By locating Ubu and Jarry in Liverpool, Henri is indicating the influence of the Surrealist tradition. This – combined with the amalgamation of Henri's daily world highlighted by the use of locations and people he knew in both the paintings and poems; and an imagined world, populated by his heroes, where they may meet on a Liverpool street – is a frequent motif employed by Henri.[85]

'Liverpool Poems' is an important early poem of Henri's as it references both popular and high culture, highlighting a postmodern aspect to Henri's work.

David Bateman notes that it was Henri's painting at this time that was directly influencing the writing of the poetry.[86] The visual images that were manifesting in the paintings and artworks were a direct result of Henri's urban locale and the influence of pop-artists such as Warhol and Jasper Johns, getting different things from either artist. The influence of the city is paramount here. Peter Barry defines the view of the poet in the city, arguing that it leaves little or no room for personal themes,

> The gaze of the poet in the city sees people, objects and vistas, and the overwhelming plenitude of things seen leaves no easy route back to personal subjectivity [...][87]

In 'Liverpool Poems', poem 8 again highlights the urban landscape, with specific landmarks and a Batman reference:

8
And I saw DEATH in Upper Duke St
Cloak flapping black tall Batman collar
Striding tall shoulders down the hill past the Cathedral
brown shoes slightly down at the heel.[88]

The image of death here may have been appropriated from the film *The Seventh Seal* (Dir. Ingmar Bergman, 1957), where God plays chess against the Grim Reaper.[89]

The Surrealism in the early poems of Henri becomes particularly apparent in poem 10 of 'Liverpool Poems':

10
Prostitutes in the snow in Canning St like strange erotic snowmen
And Marcel Proust in the Kardomah eating Madeleine butties dipped
    in tea.[90]

Though sex workers work in all weathers, the idea that scantily-clad women work in freezing temperatures, is a grim, yet accurate image, while the Proust reference itself works on different levels. Proust's epic work was *À la Recherche du Temps Perdu* published in several volumes over the course of 14 years,[91] Proust made famous the Madeleine cake, as it enables the narrator to access involuntary memory, that is, to experience his past as he experiences the present. Henri locates Proust in the Kardomah, a café in Liverpool (there were two branches, one in Stanley Street, the other in Church Street) and alters the experience that he has. By depicting Proust eating the cake on 'butties' and 'dipped in tea', Henri is making use of the local dialect here. A 'buttie' is a sandwich and the reference plays on the local legend of 'conny onny butties' which is a condensed milk sandwich. The condensed milk came in a thickened liquid form which was used to sweeten and lighten tea or coffee, and also to spread on bread. Here, Henri is domesticating the scenario and locating the European modernist experience onto the localised

Liverpool scene, leading the reader to participate in the humour of the scenario.

Another Henri poem, which takes its title from one of Henri's paintings and appears in both *The Mersey Sound* and *Tonight at Noon*, 'The Entry of Christ Into Liverpool', again mixes references to both popular and high culture. Henri's painting, subtitled on the canvas 'Homage to James Ensor', alludes to the Belgian artist, whose symbolist style was interlaced with realist images.[92] Henri, here, deliberately references Ensor's most famous painting, 'The Entry of Christ Into Brussels' (1888).[93] Walter Benjamin sees the influence of the city crowd upon Ensor, which Henri obviously uses too:

> [James Ensor] tirelessly confronted its discipline [the city's] with its wildness; he liked to put military groups in his carnival mobs, and both got along splendidly.[94]

This image also occurs in the poem. The opening stanza sets the scene for what is to follow. Interestingly, Henri brings a very urban form of nature into the cityscape, a technique that he was to continue throughout his writing career:

The Entry of Christ into Liverpool

City morning. dandelionseeds   blowing from wasteground.
smell of overgrown privethedges. children's voices
in the distance. sounds from the river.
round the corner into Myrtle St. Saturdaymorning shoppers
headscarves. shopping baskets. dogs. [95]

The use of compound words is noticeable. Perhaps this is a nod to James Joyce's use of such words in *Ulysses*. It is worth noting that this usage was a common mannerism at that time and also cropped up in the work of McGough and Patten. The sense of

calm and domesticity is located (literally) away from the action of
Christ entering Liverpool (Myrtle Street was near Henri's home,
while the event of the poem is in the city centre at St George's Hall
on Lime Street) highlighted by the layout change and the use of
capitalization and centered text:

then
   down the hill

THE SOUND OF TRUMPETS
cheering and shouting in the distance
children running
icecream vans
flags breaking out over buildings
black and red green and yellow
Union Jacks Red Ensigns
LONG LIVE SOCIALISM
stretched against the blue sky
over St George's hall [96]

The 'LONG LIVE SOCIALISM' line is a direct lift from Ensor's painting,
and is also featured in Henri's. The next stanza is introduced in a
similar way to the first with a left-justified line:

Now the procession[97]

Here Henri slows the pace of the poem, after the street party
atmosphere of the first stanza, preparing the reader for the stanza
which follows with its vivid description and colours adding to the
carnival mood. The poem is achieving something that the painting
cannot really do, which is the introduction, and concept of time.
The musical tone is set again by capitalization, indicating noise
above the volume of the street:

THE MARCHING DRUMS
hideous masked Breughel faces of old ladies in the crowd

> yellow masks of girls in curlers and headscarves
> smelling of factories
> Masks   Masks   Masks
> red masks   purple masks   pink masks[98]

Henri uses this section of the poem to differentiate between the ages of the carnival-goers: both 'girls' and 'old ladies' share the commonality of masks. This use of masks, is another allusion to Ensor, as masks featured in heavily in his paintings, for example, 'The Strange Masks' and 'Masks Confronting Death', both depicting revellers.[99] The reference to Brueghel is pertinent, as it refers back to the Ensor painting (and indeed the Henri painting) and the kind of faces that Henri was depicting. Brueghel's work is famous for scenes containing crowds, usually peasants, located in the countryside.[100]

The poem continues with references to Liverpool place names and descriptive language which colours the scene and carries the narrator towards the setting of the poem's title:

> crushing surging carrying me along
> down the hill past the Philharmonic The Labour Exchange
> excited feet crushing the geraniums in St Luke's Gardens
> placards   banners   posters
> End the War in Vietnam
> God Bless Our Pope[101]

It is important to note the words contained on the banners: the politicised call to end the Vietnam War, a contentious issue of the day; and the reference to the Pope.[102] At the time Henri was working on the poem, Liverpool was a highly sectarian city with strict divisions between the Catholics and Protestants. Henri balances the banner imagery in the following stanza by making reference to the 'embroidered banners' of the '*Loyal Sons of King William Lodge, Bootle.*'[103] The longest stanza follows. It is vivid in its language and cultural references. Interestingly, by this point in the poem, Liverpool seems to have become a more generic urban locale. The references in this stanza include Jarry again, and Guillaume Apollinaire, French poet and art critic, who experimented with spatial form and lineation in his poetry (perhaps Henri included him in this poem because of his own experiments with layout).[104]

Henri builds the momentum of Christ entering the city, by repeating the references to signs, posters and banners. Ensor reappears in the text as the maker of masks: 'J. Ensor, Fabriqueur de Masques',[105] and then the reason for the carnival gathering appears on a banner:

'HAIL JESUS, KING OF THE JEWS'[106]

The pace of the poem increases again, with the description of the view towards the returning Christ, the short phrasing and descriptive language:

red hair   white robe   grey donkey[107]

It is worth considering the fact that the poem was set to music and performed by the Henri-led band, The Liverpool Scene, appearing on their 1968 album, *Bread on the Night*.[108]

The rhythm of the poem evokes the performative element and also, the link between image and rhythm is evident too. This juxtaposition is what Catherine Marcangeli calls the 'destabilisation of the notion of description.'[109]

An interesting insight to the poem comes from Henri himself. There are a series of statements, from Henri at the end of *Tonight At Noon*, and he makes reference to the 'The Entry of Christ into Liverpool' painting:

> There is a quote from the 'The Entry of Christ into Brussels' in the LONG LIVE SOCIALISM banner. And the 'Colman's Mustard'

advert is a quote from an Ensor drawing 'Hail, Jesus, King of the Jews' of 1885 which has I think the first bit of pop art in it. In the background there is a poster for Colman's mustard.[110]

This is an important statement as both quotations appear in the poem. A recurring motif through Henri's work is that of the use of quotation. It is in evidence in both the art and the poetry.[111]

Henri runs with the pop-art imagery and cleverly replicates the flashing of neon advertising:

GUIN

GUINN

GUINNESS IS

white bird dying unnoticed in a corner

splattered feathers

blood running merged with the neonsigns

in a puddle

GUINNESS IS GOOD

GUINNESS   IS   GOOD   FOR

Masks   Masks   Masks   Masks   Masks

GUINNESS IS GOOD FOR YOU[112]

Henri returns to the domesticated scene which began the poem. The narrator is returning to the scene after the entry of Christ into Liverpool.

We may ask why Henri chose Liverpool to locate the painting and poem. Aside from the city being Henri's home, perhaps he is pointing to the cultural renaissance that was occurring in Liverpool at that time: the cultural rebirth of a city that had suffered greatly in the post-war period. Also, Liverpool was a city with a large amount of sectarianism and as such, would be a very surreal location for Christ to appear, or maybe he was there to reconcile. This stanza slows the pace highlighting the post-carnival atmosphere.[113] There are stylistic variations to the first stanza, but the overall tone of domesticity and calm is replicated, enhanced by the descriptions of the evening sky. This description is painterly in its execution, rather like a landscape being painted bit by bit:

> evening
> thin sickle moon
> pale blue sky
> flecked with bright orange clouds[114]

The narrator highlights the post-carnival atmosphere by mentioning the 'streamers newspapers discarded paper hats/blown slowly back up the hill by the evening wind' and the 'dustmen with big brooms sweeping the gutters'.[115] The narrative voice shifts register by introducing 'me' into the poem's final lines, alongside a flâneurial observation:

> me
> walking home
> empty chip-papers drifting round my feet.[116]

Another poem of Henri's contained in both *The Mersey Sound* and *Tonight at Noon* that mixes high and popular culture, literary and musical heroes alongside Henri's own friends, is 'Me'.[117] The poem uses rhythm as a device to keep the reader, or listener (Henri would have performed this poem regularly at readings and happenings that he was involved in. Catherine Marcangeli notes that he 'read it up until the end [...] I must have heard it hundreds of times.'), interested.[118] The poem is subtitled 'if you weren't you who would like to be?', immediately involving the reader/listener. This highlights the notion of communication between the poet and audience, something that was important to Henri, by the use of the pronouns 'I' and 'You'. This poem succeeds on two levels. Firstly, it points to Henri's influences and heroes, literary, musical and from the art world, such as William Burroughs, Charlie Parker and Monet, alongside his own contemporaries such as The Beatles who are all named individually, and the likes of poets Roger McGough and Adrian Mitchell. Secondly, the poem was written to be performed. It works better as a poem vocalized, due to its rhythmic construction which emphasizes the importance that Henri and the other 'Liverpool' poets such as Brian Patten and Roger McGough placed on performance poetry.

The first stanza of 'Me' establishes the mood and pace of the poem, which is maintained, aside from a rhythmic shift halfway through, in stanza six. The opening stanza reads:

> Paul McCartney Gustave Mahler
> Alfred Jarry John Coltrane
> Charlie Mingus Claude Debussy
> Wordsworth Monet Bach and Blake[119]

Metrical concerns dictate how the names appear. This is shown in the final line of the first stanza when William Wordsworth, Claude Monet, Johann Sebastian Bach and William Blake appear without their first names.

The sixth stanza also highlights this tactic of omitting first names to allow for strict rhythmic structure, as only two of the list have their complete names:

> Marx Dostoyevsky
> Bakunin Ray Bradbury
> Miles Davis Trotsky
> Stravinsky and Poe[120]

This rhythmic shift was something that Henri announced in readings. During performances he would stop reading and say, 'change of rhythm'.[121] Also of note in this stanza are the political figures that Henri names: Karl Marx, considered the founding Father of Communism; Mikhail Bakunin, a prominent figure in the Russian Socialist movement; Leon Trotsky, the Marxist revolutionary and theorist. By omitting Christian names, Henri also allows the poem to work on another level not concerning the strict metre. By choosing Communist luminaries, we get a strong sense of the poem's political sympathies.

The rhythmic structure throughout the poem also hints at the jazz blues choruses, of which many of the names listed would have practiced: Miles Davis, John Coltrane and Charlie Mingus.[122] Catherine Marcangeli notes that Donald McKinlay, who appears in the ninth stanza, was an artist friend of Henri's who was never referred to as Donald. He was always called Don. His full name was placed in the poem to fit its rigid structure.[123] Similarly, Marcangeli notes that when the poem is read aloud 'one becomes aware that the necessities of rhythm dictate the order in which the names are reeled off. For this is also a formal experiment in scansion.'[124]

The coda to the poem is interesting, as it is the first input from the narratorial voice and it matches the final stanza of 'The Entry of Christ into Liverpool' with the speaker placed on his own. Here we have a kind of understated humour and a kind of tongue in cheek modesty:

Stéphane Mallarmé and Alfred de Vigny
Ernst Mayakovsky and Nicolas de Stael
Hindemith Mick Jagger Durer and Schwitters
Garcia Lorca
                    and
                        last of all
                            me.[125]

The title poem of the collection *Tonight at Noon* highlights Henri's ability to deal with writing love poems in an often unusual style. 'Tonight at Noon' is maudlin in its conclusion yet playful in its execution. The reader is transported to an alternative universe hinted at by the title. The title as acknowledged in the poem, stems from an 'LP by Charles Mingus "Tonight at Noon", Atlantic 1416'. The poem is also dedicated to 'Charles Mingus and the Clayton Squares', a MerseyBeat band who were named after a city centre square.

'Tonight at Noon' is also the opening poem in *The Mersey Sound* further highlighting the importance that Henri and the publishers, Penguin, gave to it. Lines from the first stanza which opens with 'Tonight at noon/Supermarkets will advertise 3P EXTRA on everything', include 'Children from happy families will be sent to live in a home', 'America will declare peace on Russia', and 'the first daffodils of autumn will appear'. This form is continued throughout the poem, with its list of surrealist impossibilities, whose possibility is nonetheless, and therefore paradoxically, suggested by the certainty of 'will', alongside the perhaps inevitable reference to Liverpool: 'A tunnel full or water will be built under Liverpool/ Pigs will be sighted flying in formation over Woolton.'[126] There is also an argument that Henri was applying the surrealist practice of automatism. In the Surrealist Manifesto of 1924 André Breton suggests that surrealism is 'pure psychic automatism.'[127] With regard to writing, the manifesto states that automatism requires an affirmation. We can see this in the final lines of 'Tonight at Noon':

> In forgotten graveyards everywhere the dead will quietly bury
>   the living
> and
> You will tell me you love me
> Tonight at noon[128]

Henri's next collection, *City*, published in 1969, was a departure from the previous two collections. It is a long single poem in four distinct parts.

Henri's direct lineage of influence can be traced back past the Beats and T.S. Eliot to Charles Baudelaire. Henri will have been aware of Baudelaire's use of allegory and the poet's use of mixing the ordinary with the extraordinary as seen in allegorical poems such as 'The Swan' and 'The Seven Old Men'.[129] Just as Baudelaire was referring to the new modern world that was building around him in Paris, and as Eliot was referring back to Baudelaire, Henri appropriates the language around him: that of the billboards and the magazines as well as Eliot and Baudelaire.[130] The interesting connection between all three poets is the fact that they defamiliarize the city through their various techniques, chiefly that of allegory; to all three the city is unreal, the location of visions and mysteries; carnivals and death. *City* quotes Baudelaire in the introduction, but does not credit him; similarly the quote appears as a subtitle to Henri's introductory essay in the Peter Robinson edited collection *Liverpool Accents: Seven Poets and a City*.[131] O swarming city, city full of dreams, where ghosts accost the passers-by in broad daylight![132]

> '*Swarming city*
> city full of dreams
> where the ghost in broad daylight
> *passes by the passers-by.*'

Edinburgh Sept 1967 – Liverpool Sept 1968[133]

Tellingly, Henri gives us a clue to the composition of *City* by following his Baudelaire translation with two dates and times: *Edinburgh Sept 1967 – Liverpool Sept 1968.*

Henri's reason for not acknowledging Baudelaire may be that he translated the text himself. Henri used the quote (in an edited version) in a much later, and to-date, uncollected poem 'City 2000'. The poem appeared in an obituary by Professor John Ashton in

'The Journal of Epidemiology and Community Health', in 2002. Interestingly, Henri here is using poetry as a visual device and is referencing his painting:

> The night
> written in dripping white
> on a railway wall
> 'Swarming city, city full of dreams'[134]

Part One of *City* immediately locates the reader into the domesticity that populates the whole of the first part of the poem:

> Got up went to the telephone bought some pies and rolls for
>   lunch thinking of you tried to phone you they said you
>   weren't there came home made some coffee had my lunch
>   thinking of you.[135]

The fifteen stanzas of Part One continue with this domestic theme, clearly located, as noted by the subtitle to the whole poem, in Edinburgh, with the shift back to Liverpool in stanza twelve:

> Thinking of you trying to finish this poem back in Liverpool
>   where everyone's my friend except some of my friends
>   taking the flower painting I did for you to be framed in gold
>   like our love should be [...][136]

The repeated motif and refrain 'thinking of you' is used throughout the whole poem, as a structuring device with the intention of holding together the collage of images, snippets and impressions.

Part Two is more minimalist. Located firmly back in Liverpool, this part uses the whiteness of the page and apes the Charles Olson and William Carlos Williams sense of poetics allowing the poem to become, in Williams's words, 'a [...] small or (large) machine made out of words'[137]. Part two of the poem begins:

PART TWO

november.

the long fog echoes in from the river.

9.30

echoing schoolgirl hymnsinging voices into the mist outside
    Blackburne House

leaves.[138]

What is interesting here is the punctuation that Henri employs
to slow the pace after the speed and complexity of Part One. This
reflective tone is replicated from its content to layout.

Throughout this time, the late 1960s, Henri continued the
tradition of the Benjaminian/Baudelairean flâneur. The first record
of the term flâneur appears in 1806 in an anonymous pamphlet
titled *Le Flâneur au salon ou M. Bon-Homme: examen joyeux des
tableaux, mêlé de vaudevilles.*[139] This flâneur, the fictional M. Bon-
Homme, differs from the flâneurs that followed in the 1830s in
that his reporting was limited to travelling the same routes daily,
whilst the later flâneur was concerned with chance and a rejection
of forming plans. The flâneur was always considered to be male.[140]
The lineage of the flâneur can be traced to Jean-Jacques Rousseau's
solitary promenader, a person who walks the borders between the
urban locale and the countryside and who, according to Heinz
Paetzold, is 'confused by the urban crowd.'[141] Again, major
differences are visible. The flâneur is solely concerned with the
urban landscape and is uninterested in the notion of the non-urban.
The flâneur prefers not to become part of the crowd, but to observe
silently and alone. Rob Shields argues:

> Flânerie is a sociability of 'Ones' which emphasizes and preserves
> the separateness of the individual. As such it is a social practice of a

generalized democratic individualism which was new to nineteenth-century Europeans.[142]

Henri continued to use signifiers of the natural world in the chaos of the city; though he often used the surrealist motif of reversal, placing the extraordinary into the ordinary, culminating in the strangeness of the everyday. This is shown in the poem 'Poem In Memoriam T.S. Eliot' which appears in both *The Mersey Sound* and *Tonight at Noon* :

> The first signs of spring in plastic daffodils
> on city counters [143]

A strong theme of Henri's, as with both Eliot and Baudelaire, is the struggle of the natural world amongst the evolving and ever present city: the bird in the city, dead unnoticed; 'blood running merged with the neonsigns in a puddle';[144] 'the daffodils trodden underfoot';[145] and 'excited feet crushing the geraniums in St Lukes Gardens'.[146] Catherine Marcangeli concurs with this viewpoint:

> ANDREW TAYLOR: A lot of the painting feeds into the poetry and the poetry feeds into the painting. There is a lot of the natural world in the paintings and in the poetry, even a lot of the 'urban' poems like 'Poem for Liverpool 8' there are a lot of smells like lilac and honeysuckle, it's not just the chip wrappers and the litter bins.
> CATHERINE MARCANGELI: I think it's the weed that's coming through the paving cracks as well. A neighbour had a honeysuckle and walking home at night, he could smell it.[147]

Towards the end of the 1960s, Henri would spend time further time away from Liverpool touring with the band The Liverpool Scene. Henri was the singer and the band performed musical versions of poems of his such as 'Love Is', 'The Entry of Christ into Liverpool' and 'Batpoem'. They toured with Led Zeppelin and played dates in America where Henri would meet up again with

Allen Ginsberg and his poetry would, through travel and reflection, take on a different mode.

In his book, *The Liverpool Scene*, Lucie-Smith allows the poets space to introduce themselves and talk about their work. The exception is Allen Ginsberg whose work does not appear in the book, despite his rear cover blurb. However, the following aforementioned quote in its entirety adds credence to Johan Raskin's argument that Ginsberg wished to sound sage-like:

> ... Liverpool, which I think is at the present moment the centre of the consciousness of the human universe. They're resurrecting the human form divine there – all those beautiful youths with long, golden archangelic hair.[148]

Henri gives us further clues to his poetics, influences and technique in the text, 'Notes on Painting and Poetry'.[149] Interestingly, he points to the rise in communications technology and gives a clue to his practice of collaging:

> I think my concern should be with the whole area of language as it impinges on me, now. Because we live in an era of communications-explosion, certain specialist uses of language seem particularly relevant: that of advertising (hoardings, slogans, tv ads) or newspaper headlines, where the aim is to establish a word/sound pattern in the memory as quickly as possible. Both demand considerable economy of means and a rethinking of ideas about syntax.[150]

Henri used quotations from both Baudelaire and Eliot in his work. Though prone to using a list technique of names and heroes in his poetry, Henri clearly accepted the tradition of 'city' poets who had gone before:

> I cannot imagine what it would have been like to be a poet and not live here [Liverpool]; or, indeed, whether I would have become a poet at all. From Baudelaire, Apollinaire and Eliot onwards the city

has haunted the poetic imagination. This city continues to haunt mine.[151]

Henri, like Eliot and Baudelaire was not without his critics. Baudelaire's poetry at its time of composition and publication was considered shocking to the extent that certain poems originally planned for inclusion in *Les Fleurs du Mal* (*The Flowers of Evil*), were banned. Eliot's *The Waste Land*, too, was considered scandalous upon its publication. J.C. Squire said of the *The Waste Land*:

> Its apparent object being to reflect in a vagrant and fatigued sequence of images the exhaustion of our civilisation. The mood is familiar enough: it is what thirty years ago they used to call 'fin-de-siècle': Baudelaire without his guts. It is a dyspeptic mood, the mood of a man of low vitality, a man feeling 'below par'.
>
> The diagnosis on which it is nominally founded seems to me unsound.[152]

Henri and the other 'Liverpool Poets' were all attacked by various critics, including Douglas Dunn who argued:

> [they] represent an unliterary principle of making poems, subordinating craft to effect, [and are] small town demotic Mantovanis endorsing sentiments and expectations they have no need to create.[153]

Contemporary critics are often short sighted when it comes to the poetry that is seen as 'new'. Henri was at the frontline of something new in British poetry as *The Mersey Sound* and these early collections show.

Notes

[55]Birkenhead was then in the county of Cheshire, it is now part of Merseyside. It is known locally as 'over the water'.

[56]Bateman, 'Adrian Henri: Singer of Meat and Flowers' in *Gladsongs and Gatherings: Poetry and its social context in Liverpool since the 1960s*, ed. Stephen Wade (Liverpool: Liverpool University Press, 2001), p73.

[57]Adrian Henri interview with David Bateman in Steven Wade ed. *Gladsongs and Gatherings*, p81.

[58]The interview with Catherine Marcangeli took place on 30 May 2005, at the Mount Street home in Liverpool that she shared with Adrian Henri.

[59]Adrian Henri, *City* (London: Rapp and Whiting, 1968). The cover design was by Lawrence Edwards. The idea is clearly from Henri, as the streets which spell city from the *A-Z* map, includes Mount Street, where Henri lived and Hope Street where he worked at the College of Art.

[60]Debord defined the *dérive* in an essay published in *Internationale Situationniste # 2* in December 1958. In the paper, Debord acknowledges that the '*dérive* is one of the basic situationist practices' and further points to it being 'a technique of rapid passage through varied ambiences [involving] playful-constructive behaviour and awareness of psychogeographical effects. Guy Debord, 'Theory of the Dérive', *Internationale Situationniste #2* (December 1958) trans. Ken Knabb, undated, The Bureau of Public Secrets, http://www.bopsecrets.org April 1 2006 <http://www.bopsecrets.org/SI/2.derive.htm.>

[61]This focus on the city was primarily due to the success of The Beatles from 1963 and following their American tour of 1964, but Liverpool had had a burgeoning beat poetry and jazz scene from the early 1960s.

[62]Darren Pih, 'Liverpool's Left Bank' in Grunenberg and Knifton, eds, *Centre of the Creative Universe*, p118. Phil Bowen, too, describes the Beaulieu Jazz Festival as an important precursor to the bohemian Liverpool scene. See 'The Fifties and the Beginning of the Liverpool Scene' in Bowen, *A Gallery to Play To: The Story of The Mersey Poets*, pp15-17, for more about the influence of the festival.

[63]For more about Sampson and Barlow's see David Bateman's interview

with Adrian Henri 'Singer of Meat and Flowers' in Stephen Wade ed. *Gladsongs and Gatherings*, pp87-88.

[64]Darren Pih, 'Liverpool's Left Bank' in Grunenberg and Knifton, eds, *Centre of the Creative Universe*, p114.

[65]Ibid, pp115-117.

[66]Ibid, footnote 2, p114. Difficulties with definition of areas within Liverpool, continues today. There is the Mathew Street Quarter, obviously centred on Mathew Street where the Cavern Club was and where the 'new' Cavern stands; the Ropewalks area which runs from the Seel Street area to the Bold Street area and the new Baltic Triangle area. The Baltic Triangle is the new designated area where artists are encouraged to house their studios, as the city-centre rents are now too high. The area is centred on Greenland Street, Jamaica Street and Jordan Street.

[67]Adrian Henri, 'Liverpool 8' in *Collected Poems* (London: Allison and Busby, 1986), p58. 'Liverpool 8' first appeared in Edward Lucie-Smith, ed, *The Liverpool Scene* (New York: Doubleday, 1968), p23.

[68]Chronology in *Adrian Henri: Paintings 1953-1998* (Liverpool: National Museums and Galleries on Merseyside, 2000), p135.

[69]Email from Catherine Marcangeli to the author, 20 November 2017.

[70]The School of Art building on Hope Street has been sold by Liverpool John Moores University to property developers.

[71]See 'Liverpool 1957-1961' in Bowen, *A Gallery to Play To*, p35, for more about Ye Cracke.

[72]Simon Warner, 'Raising the Consciousness? Re-visiting Allen Ginsberg's Liverpool Trip in 1965' in Grunenberg and Knifton, eds, *Centre of the Creative Universe*, p105.

[73]Adrian Henri in *Liverpool Accents: Seven Poets and a City,* ed. Peter Robinson (Liverpool: Liverpool University Press, 1996), p36.

[74]Adrian Henri, 'Liverpool Poems' in *Collected Poems* (London: Allison and Busby, 1986), p30. I have sourced Henri's work from the *Collected Poems* and cross referenced them with the individual volumes to check

for variations, including the *Selected and Unpublished Poems 1965-2000*, ed. Catherine Marcangeli (Liverpool: Liverpool University Press, 2007). 'Liverpool Poems' first appeared in Adrian Henri, Roger McGough and Brian Patten, *The Mersey Sound* (London: Penguin, 1967), pp31-33, and in Henri's first collection of poetry, *Tonight at Noon* (London: Rapp and Whiting, 1968), pp15-16. It is considered important enough to appear in *Adrian Henri: Selected and Unpublished 1965-2000*, ed. Catherine Marcangeli (Liverpool: Liverpool University Press, 2007), pp102-103.

[75]Biographical information sourced from the Guggenheim Collection, online. Undated. 3 April 2006 http://www.guggenheimcollection.org/site/artist_bio_23.html

[76]Email from Catherine Marcangeli, 20 November 2017.

[77]For further information regarding Adrian Henri's art, perhaps the best resource is the catalogue from the exhibition titled *Adrian Henri: Paintings 1953-1998* (Liverpool: National Museums and Galleries on Merseyside, 2000), see pp62-3 and pp66-7.

[78]Adrian Henri, 'Liverpool Poems' in *Collected Poems*, p30.

[79]Ibid.

[80]Ibid.

[81]Wikipedia.org, undated. http://www.en.wikipedia.org/wiki/Licensing_laws_of_the_United_Kingdom 4 April 2006

[82]Adrian Henri, 'Liverpool Poems' in *Collected Poems*, p30. Yates Wine Lodge is the brand name of a pub chain popular throughout Britain. At the time Henri wrote the poem, Yates Wine Lodge were low market establishments with sawdust on the floor.

[83]Ibid.

[84]Alfred Jarry is an important predecessor of the Absurdist Theatre. His UBU ROI (1896) is a mythical figure, set amidst a world of grotesque archetypal images. Ubu Roi is a caricature, a terrifying image of the animal nature of man and his cruelty. (Ubu Roi makes himself King of Poland and kills and tortures all and sundry. The work is a puppet play and its décor of childish naivety emphasizes the horror.) Jarry expressed

man's psychological states by objectifying them on the stage. The University of Glasgow, Faculty of Arts, undated, http:// www.arts.gla.ac.uk/faculty/ 4 April 2006, http://www.arts.gla.ac.uk/ Slavonic/Absurd.htm. For more information regarding Jarry's work see Claude Schumacher's *Alfred Jarry and Guillaume Apollinaire* (London: Macmillan 1984) and *Alfred Jarry: The Ubu Plays* trans. by Cyril Connolly and Simon Watson Taylor (London: Methuen, 1976).

[85]The poem 'The Entry of Christ into Liverpool' and painting of the same name, are good examples of this technique. See below for more on this poem/painting.

[86]David Bateman, 'Adrian Henri: Singer of Meat and Flowers' in *Gladsongs and Gatherings*, p76.

[87]Peter Barry, *Contemporary British Poetry and the City* (Manchester: Manchester University Press, 2000), p224.

[88]Adrian Henri, 'Liverpool Poems' in *Collected Poems*, p31.

[89]International Movie Database, undated, http://www.imdb.com 4 April 2006 http://www.imdb.com/title/tt0050976

[90]Adrian Henri, 'Liverpool Poems' in *Collected Poems*, p31.

[91]For more information on Proust, see Jean Yves Tadié's *Marcel Proust: A Life,* trans. by Euan Cameron (London: Penguin, 2000).

[92]For more information on James Ensor, visit the Boston College Website, undated, http://www.bc.edu/ 4 April 2006 http://www.bc.edu/bc_org/ avp/cas/fnart/art/ensor.html

[93]See *Adrian Henri: Paintings 1953-1998* (Liverpool: National Museums and Galleries on Merseyside, 2000), pp58-61.

[94]Walter Benjamin, *Illuminations*, trans. by Harry Zohn (London: Fontana, 1973), p176.

[95]Adrian Henri, 'The Entry of Christ Into Liverpool' in *Collected Poems*, p69. The poem first appeared in Adrian Henri, Roger McGough and Brian Patten, *The Mersey Sound*, pp46-48 and in *Adrian Henri: Selected and Unpublished 1965-2000,* ed, Catherine Marcangeli, pp. 99-101.

[96]Adrian Henri, 'The Entry of Christ Into Liverpool' in *Collected Poems*, p69.

[97]Ibid.

[98]Ibid.

[99]See the Museum of Modern Art website, undated http://www.moma.org 6 April 2006 http://www.moma.org/collection/ browse_results.php?object_id=79855

[100]For more on Brueghel visit the ABC Gallery website, undated http:// www.abcgallery.com 5 April 2006 http://www.abcgallery.com/B/ bruegel/pieterbio.html. The spelling of Brueghel sometimes appears as Breugel, information accessed on-line at WebMuseum Paris 16 August 2002 http://www.ibiblio.org 7 April 2007 http://www.ibiblio.org/wm/ paint/auth/bruegel.

[101]Adrian Henri, 'The Entry of Christ into Liverpool' in *Collected Poems*, p69.

[102]In the painting, the internationally recognised peace sign, used by the Campaign for Nuclear Disarmament (CND) is present. See *Adrian Henri: Paintings 1953-1998*, pp58-61.

[103]Adrian Henri, 'The Entry of Christ into Liverpool' in *Collected Poems*, p69.

[104]Henri's typological experiments with the poem were made into a poster. The poster appeared in Henri's retrospective exhibition at Liverpool Walker Art Gallery, 4 February-2 April 2000 and at the exhibition, 'The Centre of the Creative Universe: Liverpool and the Avant-Garde' at Tate Liverpool that ran from 20 February-9 September 2007. The poster did not appear in the exhibition catalogue.

[105]Adrian Henri, 'The Entry of Christ into Liverpool' in *Collected Poems*, p70.

[106]Ibid.

[107]Ibid.

[108]The Liverpool Scene, *Bread on the Night* (London: RCA Victor Records SF8057, 1968).

[109]Email from Catherine Marcangeli to the author, 20 November 2017.

Adrian Henri, 'About Images' in 'Notes on Painting and Poetry' in *Tonight at Noon*, p72.

[110]I have researched the origins of Colman's mustard and have ascertained that the mustard was in existence at the time of Ensor's drawing: the company was established in 1814. Information gathered from Colman's New Zealand website undated http://www.colmanfoods.co.za/ 6 April 2006 http://www.colmanfoods.co.za/history.asp.

[111]If we take 'Mrs Albion, You've Got a Lovely Daughter' as an example, we can see the use of quotation and allusion as Henri uses song lyrics from Herman's Hermits, 'Mrs Brown, You've a Lovely Daughter', Chuck Berry, 'Reelin' and Rockin'' and Dusty Springfield's version of the Hal David and Burt Bacharach song, 'Wishin' and Hopin''. Later poems that incorporated quotations included 'New York City Blues' (for John Lennon) which directly quotes from a famous Lennon Lyric: 'Life is what happens to you when you're busy making other plans.' Adrian Henri, 'Mrs Albion, You've Got a Lovely Daughter' in *Collected Poems*, pp53-54, and Adrian Henri, 'New York City Blues' from *Penny Arcade* in *Collected Poems*, p304.

[112]Adrian Henri, 'The Entry of Christ into Liverpool' in *Collected Poems*, p70.

[113]This carnival atmosphere hints again at Père Ubu who appears in the painting but not the poem 'The Entry of Christ into Liverpool'. See footnote 42.

[114]Adrian Henri, 'The Entry of Christ into Liverpool' in *Collected Poems*, p70.

[115]Ibid.

[116]Ibid, p71.

[117]Adrian Henri, 'Me' in *Collected Poems*, p1. The poem also appears in Adrian Henri, Roger McGough and Brian Patten, *The Mersey Sound*, pp44-45, and in Adrian Henri, *Selected and Unpublished 1965-2000*, ed. Catherine Marcangeli, pp201-202.

[118]Email from Catherine Marcangeli to the author, 10 November 2017.

[119]Adrian Henri, 'Me' in *Collected Poems*, p1.

[120]Ibid.

[121]Email from Catherine Marcangeli to the author, 10 November 2017. Marcangeli likens it to the changing of sides when an LP is turned over.

[122]This structure is similar to the method used by Jack Kerouac in his 'Blues' poems. See Kerouac's *Book of Blues* (New York: Penguin Poets, 2005).

[123]Interview by the author with Catherine Marcangeli took place on 7 July 2007, at the Mount Street home in Liverpool that she shared with Adrian Henri. Don McKinley also appears in Henri's painting 'The Entry of Christ Into Liverpool', see *Adrian Henri: Paintings 1953-1998*, p60.

[124]Catherine Marcangeli in *Adrian Henri: Total Artist* (London: Occasional Papers, 2014), p5.

[125]Adrian Henri, 'Me' in *Collected Poems*, p2.

[126]Adrian Henri, 'Tonight at Noon' in *The Mersey Sound*, p11.

[127]Suzanne Guerlac, *Literary Polemics* (Redwood City: Stanford University Press, 1997), p236. Catherine Marcangeli notes that 'Breton's automatism is a way of accessing the unconscious. With Adrian, it's a different kind of process, and aim. It's more to do with the deliberate collage of impossibilities.' Email from Catherine Marcangeli to the author, 10 November 2017.

[128]Adrian Henri, 'Tonight at Noon' in *The Mersey Sound*, p12.

[129]'The Swan', in Charles Baudelaire, *The Complete Verse Volume I*, trans. by Francis Scarfe (London and Wolfeboro NH: Anvil Press Poetry, 1986), p174; 'The Seven Old Men' in Baudelaire, *The Complete Verse Volume I*, p177.

[130]See footnote 67.

[131]Adrian Henri, 'A City of Poems' in Robinson ed. *Liverpool Accents: Seven Poets and a City*, p35. Regarding the title of the poem, Henri will have been aware of Roy Fisher's important text about Birmingham,

'City', first published in 1961 and later collected in *The Dow Low Drop: New and Selected Poems* (Newcastle Upon Tyne: Bloodaxe, 1996). See also Robert Sheppard, *The Poetry of Saying: British Poetry and its Discontents, 1950-2000* (Liverpool: Liverpool University Press, 2004), pp77-81; and Peter Barry, *Contemporary British Poetry and the City* (Manchester: Manchester University Press, 2001), pp193-218. Also, note the influence that Henri's Happenings in Liverpool had on his poetry.

[132] Baudelaire, 'The Seven Old Men' in *The Complete Verse Volume I*, p177.

[133] Adrian Henri, 'City' in *Collected Poems*, p98.

[134] Adrian Henri, 'City 2000', uncollected poem, published in 'The Death of an Artist: Adrian Henri, 1932-2000' in *The Journal of Epidemiology and Community Healthcare*, Vol 56. pp72-75. Article accepted for publication 23 August 2001. http://www.jech.bmjjournals.com/ 6 April 2006. http://www.jech.bmjjournals.com/cgi/content/full/56/1/72#R7

[135] Adrian Henri, 'City' in *Collected Poems*, p98.

[136] Adrian Henri 'City' in *Collected Poems*, p100.

[137] William Carlos Williams introduction to 'The Wedge' in *Selected Essays of William Carlos Williams* (New York: New Directions, 1969), p256.

[138] Adrian Henri, 'City' in *Collected Poems*, p101. It is worth noting that Blackburne House was a girls' school near Henri's home in Mount Street in Liverpool.

[139] Priscilla Parkhurst Ferguson, in *The Flâneur*, ed. Keith Tester (London: Routledge, 1994), p26.

[140] Janet Wolff argues that the 'world of the flâneur was a masculine one'. See her chapter 'The Artist and the Flâneur' in *The Flâneur*, pp111-132.

[141] Heinz Paetzold, 'The Philosophical Notion of the City' in *The City Cultures Reader*, eds. Malcolm Miles, Tim Hall and Iain Borden (London: Routledge 2000), p214.

[142] Rob Shields, in *The Flâneur*, p64.

[143]Adrian Henri, 'Poem In Memoriam T.S. Eliot' in *Collected Poems*, p92.

[144]Adrian Henri, 'The Entry of Christ into Liverpool' in *Collected Poems*, p70.

[145]Ibid.

[146]Adrian Henri, 'The Entry of Christ into Liverpool' in *Collected Poems*, p69.

[147]Interview by the author with Catherine Marcangeli, 30 May 2005, at the Mount Street home in Liverpool that she had shared with Adrian Henri.

[148]Allen Ginsberg in Edward Lucie-Smith, ed. *Liverpool Scene*, p25.

[149]Adrian Henri, 'Notes on Painting and Poetry' in *Tonight at Noon*, p76.

[150]Ibid.

[151]Adrian Henri, 'A City of Poems', in Robinson, ed. *Liverpool Accents: Seven Poets and a City*, p38.

[152]Michael Grant, ed. *T.S. Eliot: The Critical Heritage, Vol I* (Oxford: Routledge, 1982), p240.

[153]Douglas Dunn, quoted in Phil Bowen, *A Gallery to Play To*, p7.

2

THE 1970s, TRAVEL,

THERE AND BACK AGAIN

Poems for Wales and Six Landscapes for Susan (1970),
Autobiography (1971), *America* (1972)
and *Haiku* (1975)

THE EARLY 1970S WAS A TIME of reflection for Henri. The late
1960s had been a busy time. His poetry/rock band, The Liverpool
Scene, had been touring extensively, building on the success of
albums *The Amazing Adventures of The Liverpool Scene* (1968)[154]
and *Bread on the Night* (1969).[155] There was a Liverpool Scene
performance at the 1969 Isle of Wight Music Festival, sharing the
bill with Bob Dylan and bands such as Pentangle and The Band,
and a trip to America in 1969, which resulted in the writing of the
long poem *America*, later published in 1972.

Such activity, clearly good fun for Henri, living a rock band
lifestyle, perhaps had a more important role in gathering material
for poems. 1970 was to be a terrible year for him: The Liverpool
Scene broke up in early 1970 due to the usual things that split
bands up, debts and bad management.[156] Then in May and June,
Henri's maternal grandparents and his parents all died. During
August of that year, while at the Edinburgh Festival, he suffered a
mild heart attack.

Realising that most of his recent creative output had been used for The Liverpool Scene, there was now the opportunity for Henri to focus on his poetry and art. The first publication of the new decade was *Poems for Wales and Six Landscapes for Susan* published by Arc Publications as a pamphlet. As the title suggests, the pamphlet is divided into two sections, with accompanying illustrations by Margaret Mitchell. It is worth noting that 'Poems for Wales' and 'Six Landscapes for Susan' are included in Henri's *Collected Poems 1967-1985* published in 1986 by Allison & Busby, but only 'Poems for Wales' appears in *Selected and Unpublished Poems* edited by Catherine Marcangeli and published by Liverpool University Press in 2007.

The pamphlet opens with 'Six Landscapes for Susan'. These short-numbered vignettes (number 6 is the longest at nine lines) stylistically hint at the later pamphlet *Haiku*, published in 1976. If we look at section 2 of 'Six Landscapes for Susan' in its entirety, this is evident, with its overtures to nature:

2
Pools by factories applegreen
and bright with rainbows[157]

With a painterly eye, Henri takes us on a journey with the dedicatee of the poem/s. There is an overarching sense of nature within the poem/s. Part 1 has us witness 'you/in the country/looking at horses' while part 3 replicates a journey on a 'slow doubledecker bus/moving between/red dead mountain bracken'[158] Images of the natural world mix with personal memory and sounds, shown in the use of plosives, and allow us into the minutiae of these landscapes with Susan. From the final two lines of the four line part 5, this mix is evident:

pale pink roses picked for you
after pie and chips in the latenight Oldham café[159]

'Poems for Wales' is similarly laid out in individual parts. Wales was important to Henri and with its proximity to Liverpool, is in easy reach. Part 1 of the poem locates us firmly in the landscape that would have been familiar to Henri:[160]

> icegreen
>   mountain streams
>   fresher
>   than toothpaste
>   cleaner tasting
>   than menthol cigarettes[161]

The combination of manufactured freshness, in the form of toothpaste and the 'clean' taste of the cigarettes, with the real freshness, is particularly robust.

These poems would have made a fitting contribution to Henri's debut collection *Tonight at Noon*. They offer a mix of the personal and the observational with references to the Vietnam War, as does the earlier poem 'Batpoem' that appeared both in *The Mersey Sound* and *Tonight at Noon*.[162] Henri's poem 'as part 2' notes:

> 2 Gelert's grave
>   used to make me cry like a baby
>   now
>   they're killing Vietnamese
>   instead[163]

Gelert is a mythical Welsh story that led to the naming of the town of Beddgelert, where the dog of the myth is allegedly buried. This faithful dog is killed in anger by his master after he thought that the dog had killed his child. Only upon killing the dog does the master realise his error and sees the baby behind the upturned cradle. The dog is buried and its master, Prince Llywelyn of Gwynedd, never speaks again after burying the dog. There is no historical evidence that this occurred. However, the Vietnam War was certainly real and ongoing. This is also, perhaps, a reaction to Henri's childhood memories. One of the first memories he had as a child in Birkenhead, was seeing the 'river Mersey on fire', during the attacks on Liverpool during World War II.[164]

The final poem in 'Poems for Wales', would also have fitted comfortably in Henri's selection in *The Mersey Sound* or *Tonight at Noon.* It is reminiscent of those short instant poems that make up 'Liverpool Poems'[165] or 'Piccadilly Poems'[166] It is worth citing in its entirety, with the first and last words of the poem summing up the scenario; how the reader sees the shift from 'two' to 'one', the couple to the lone figure of the poet:

> 5   two lots of footprints
>   through the snow
>   to my room
>   both of them
>   mine[167]

Snow makes an appearance in part 3 of the poem, alongside painterly references; after 'looking at the landscape', the poem's narrator signs 'it at the bottom/in the snow on a petrol-station wall'.[168] This highlights the relationship between Henri's practice as a painter that influences the writing of the poetry. In the introduction to his *Collected Poems*, Henri noted that his 'work as a painter has affected my writing, and vice versa.'[169] This was to continue throughout his career.

Autobiography, published by Jonathan Cape in 1971, is in part what Henri calls a research project, 'into the person I was at each stage, [between 1932-64] using old photographs, letters, notebooks and unpublished poems from which a number of words and images were taken.'[170] Interestingly, Henri notes that '[he] found [he] could not say anything fresh about my life 1964-70, possibly because it is already too well-documented in existing published work.'[171]

It is clear that the book and its constituent parts were written as catharsis, a move away from his more recognisable style of writing and its pop-art association. *Autobiography* is a slight volume, at 46 pages, and its central subject is memory. The book is dedicated to his recently deceased relatives.[172] Part One is preceeded by a prose poem, the form of which conveys the feeling of faltering and hesitant memory, concerning a visit by the poet to his failing grandparents and their home, with its 'filthy littered/unfamiliar corridor I know from childhood out into daylight./grass growing between the cracked pavingstones.'[173] Part One, subtitled 1932-51, is in fifteen parts and deals with childhood memories. Perhaps most interesting is number four: 'Rhyl Sands'. In 1938 Henri moved with his parents to the North Wales resort of Rhyl after his father became an events organiser at a holiday camp. He would remain there until 1951, leaving for King's College in Newcastle to study fine art.

'Rhyl Sands' offers a perspective not only of place, but of the influence of art. Henri name checks artist David Cox and his painting 'Rhyl Sands'. Writing in his introduction to *Adrian Henri: Paintings 1953-1998*, Frank Milner notes how Henri would return from Newcastle by coach and while waiting for a connecting train in Manchester, would wander the city's galleries.[174] Clearly Cox's painting was a favourite of Henri's and later in 1962 Henri also produced a picture titled 'Rhyl Sands'.[175] The poem, after describing beach vistas, brings the reader's attention to:

> pebbles underfoot as clear as the wallpaper in seaside cafés[176]

Within the same stanza Henri references the Cox painting, before locating the reader back to the seaside environment of Rhyl:

> David Cox's 'Rhyl Sands' a tiny gem burning quietly in dirty
>   Manchester
> ghostly echoes of last season's chip-papers in the drifting sand[177]

Autobiography is punctuated by poems that are italicised, primarily to highlight them as contemporaneous poems that are placed outside of the timespan that each section hosts. The penultimate poem in Part Two, 1951-7, is one such example. 'Poem for Liverpool 8' returns the reader to familiar Henri territory.

This poem looks at that area of the city from two different perspectives, in two sections.[178] The first section of the poem is in the form of a fond reminiscence of the area with its combination of music, colour: ('brightgreen', 'redpurple' and 'ochre'), alongside the 'children's laughter in summer'; while the second half of the poem deals with the decay falling upon the area with its 'Georgian pediments peeling above toothless windows'.[179] The poem is typeset in italics throughout aside from two introductory lines in capitals at the beginning of each section of the poem:

> Poem for Liverpool 8
>
> LIVERPOOL 8:
> *blaze of trumpets from basement record players*
> *loud guitars in the afternoon*
> *knowing every inch of little St Bride St*
> *brightgreen patches of mildew redpurple bricks stained ochre plaster*
> *huge hearts names initials kisses painted on backdoors* [...][180]

We can see in this opening section that Henri is evoking the atmosphere of Liverpool 8 and locating the reader immediately in the area with the reference to Little St Bride Street. This street runs from Catharine Street and its Georgian terraces to Bedford Street. However, Catherine Marcangeli states that for readers familiar with the geography of Liverpool, the place and street names evoked familiar locations. For other readers, though, those names give the poem a specificity, a feel of reality.[181]

In the first section of 'Poem for Liverpool 8', street names and locations are abundant, 'Catherine Street' [sic], 'St James Rd' and 'Falkner Sq Gardens heaped with red leaves to kick in autumn.'[182] The famous Liverpool 8 landmarks of Ye Cracke ('The Cracke' in the poem); and 'the crowded cutglass Philharmonic drunk in noisy Jukebox O'Connor's' also appear.[183] Again, the first part of the poem highlights Henri's preoccupation with nature's integration with the urban environment. This is evident with Henri's use of the elements in lines such as 'pigeons disappearing at eyelevel into the mist', 'black willows into cold mist', 'bushes railings pillowed with snow in winter', and 'shattered yellowgreen with sunlight'.[184]

The tone changes significantly within the second part of the poem. The opening line of this section, again capitalized, locates the reader back to the poem's location:

> LIVERPOOL 8:
> *now a wasteland*
> *murdered by planners not German bombers* [185]

This sets the tone for the rest of this much shorter section. Unlike the first section, there is a sense of darkness and disorder highlighted by a vivid description of the creation of St James Garden in the cemetery behind the Anglican Cathedral:[186]

> *the tumbledown graveyard under the Cathedral*
> *where we kissed behind the willowtrees*
> *bulldozed into tidy gardens*
> *huge tornup roots of trees*
> *pink sandstone from uprooted walls glittering in pale sunlight*[187]

Henri reworks the situations and the atmospheres that are evident in the first section of the poem and carries them into the second section. The Cathedral is mentioned in both sections, as are children. In the first section the Cathedral has its bells ringing, whilst in the second section it is yet another site of decay, with the bulldozing of the cemetery. The children in the first section are laughing: 'noisy with children's laughter in summer' while in the second they are conspicuous by their absence: 'no happy dirtyfaced children littering the sidestreets', and 'only a distant echo of their laughter across the bonfire fireengine debris.[188] The emphasis in tone is foregrounded here by comparing the final line of the first section: 'smiling landlord on the doorstep huge in shirtsleeves and braces', suggesting laughter and frivolity, with the 'distant echo' of them in the final line.

A companion poem, again in a similar vein, is 'Poem for Summer 1967'.[189] It is worth taking into consideration that Summer 1967 was recognised as the Summer of Love. This moniker was used to identify the movement of hippies and teenagers who were railing against Capitalism and Cold War-era America. San Francisco and New York City with the areas of Haight Ashbury and Greenwich Village, respectively, were centres of this new sense of awareness. The summer arguably reached its height with the Monterey Pop Festival that took place in June of 1967. The soundtrack single to that summer was 'San Francisco (Be Sure to Wear Flowers in Your Hair)' by Scott McKenzie. In the poem, a clearly nostalgic tone is present, and that it was very much written after the fact:

> *Scott McKenzie singing 'San Francisco'*
> *nostalgic now further away than The White Cliffs of Dover*
> *[...]*
> *Tony and I picking nasturtiums for our hair*
> *in the darksmelling summer garden*
> *faraway summer gone for ever* [190]

References to Liverpool and visits from poets such as Robert Creeley and Allen Ginsberg give further evidence of the sense of nostalgia mixed with a certain sense of domesticity and humour:

> *Allen singing washing the morning dishes*
> *Bob Creeley laughing at the cardboard I put in my shoes to keep the*
>   *rain out*[191]

The next publication to appear from Henri, *America*, swiftly followed *Autobiography* in 1972. *America* was published in an edition of four hundred and published by Turret Books, a small London press. The book, with its brown square format, indicative of a Government agency file, is marked 'SECRET' in red, and alerts the reader to the following information: 'SUBJECT: America; AGENT: Adrian Henri', and Henri's Mount Street address and telephone number are given in the form of an official looking stamp. Though the poems contained in *America* are published in the *Collected Poems*, there is a different format used for the Turret Books edition. Each poem is housed on its own page, regardless of length. This is perhaps a nod to the poetics of William Carlos Williams:

> To make two bold statements: There's nothing sentimental about a machine, and: A poem is a small (or large) machine made out of words. When I say there's nothing sentimental about a poem, I mean that there can be no part that is redundant.
>
> Prose may carry a load of ill-defined matter like a ship. But poetry is a machine which drives it, pruned to a perfect economy. As in all machines, its movement is intrinsic, undulant, a physical more than a literary character.[192]

It is interesting to note that Henri acknowledged the influence of Williams, Charles Olson and the Black Mountain School in a statement of his poetics. Writing in an introduction to his poems in *Liverpool Accents: Seven Poets and a City*, Henri offers the following insight into his poetics:

> My whole poetics had been formed from the concept (ultimately derived from Williams, Olson and the Black Mountain poets) of writing for, and in one's own voice.[193]

America is made up of thirty-three pages containing twenty-nine poems and is, typical of small press publications of the time, unnumbered. Henri dedicated twelve of these poems to friends or heroes such as Apollinaire, Ted Joans, Moondog and Allen Ginsberg. In a short untitled poem, dedicated to Ginsberg, we see Henri on familiar territory, continuing his interest in writing the city, in this case, New York. The opening lines of this poem convey the scene of Ginsberg being a guide around the city. Perhaps they were on a drunken dérive?

> Allen stumbling walk guide to the nightworld
> buying egg creams at the allnight Gem Spa
> dirty faded sign FIVE-SPOT
> trashcans car engines mattresses [...][194]

This poem can also be seen as a companion poem to 'Mrs Albion, You've Got a Lovely Daughter', the poem that Henri wrote and dedicated to Ginsberg during his Liverpool visit in 1965. That poem with its puns and loans from popular songs of the time such as Herman's Hermits 'Mrs Brown, You've Got a Lovely Daughter' and 'Wishin' and Hopin'' sung by Dusty Springfield, was written after Henri and his boss at the College of Art, Arthur Ballard, escorted Ginsberg on a tour of Liverpool. Henri wrote the poem after pondering whether William Blake's notion of the Daughters of Albion was founded on the four major rivers of the country. Henri took the Mersey to be one of the rivers. The opening line of the poem, 'Albion's most lovely daughter sat on the banks of the/ Mersey dangling her landing stage in the water', is according to Henri, 'a direct reference to William Blake. So, on the one hand, it's a joke: it's about Herman's Hermits and so on; it's also about Liverpool girls, an admiring poem about the way they carry on.'[195]

It is easy to treat *America* as a long poem. In the *Collected Poems* its layout does nothing to highlight the fact that it is a series of short poems. Perhaps, though, it is the fact that most poems are dated with a fixed location that points to the travelogue nature of the work. After the dedication in the form of a statement to Bertholt Brecht: 'A confidential Report to Dr Bertolt Brecht on the Present Condition of the United States of America', we find a sarcastic quotation by Brecht himself:

> '*America, fabulous meltingpot!*
> *God's own country!*
> *Just called by the initials,*
> *USA,*
> *Like everybody's boyhood friend, incapable of change!*'
> — Bert Brecht, 'Vanished Glory
> of New York the Giant City'[196]

The collection begins with an italicised titled piece called '*TWA Flight 707 1300 hrs from London arr. NY 4.30*' dated 12.IV.69. This two-line introductory piece sets in motion the notion of a series of travel poems as Henri crisscrossed his way across the USA. The final piece is located in Detroit and dated 6.XI.69. Though not linear, we can trace Henri's movements by using his dating system throughout September, October and November of 1969. The opening poem of the sequence is distinct with it being dated to April. The Liverpool Scene's tour of the USA began in September, with their final album, *St Adrian and Co, Broadway and 3rd* with a cover designed by Henri, following in 1970.

The non-linear approach is somewhat problematic. If we look at two of the early poems/parts of the poem, dated 14.XI.69 and 13.XI.69, there seems to be no real reason for them not to be linear. '14.XI.69' is a single line, usefully setting up the scene that greets the poet upon arrival in Manhattan:

> terrible heat like an oven between the buildings[197]

The longer '13.XI.69' adds a certain sense of location mixed with humour characteristic of Henri's mid-60s work:

> On Broadway
> 3 black prostitutes
> beautiful
> standing like the Supremes
> about to sing 'Stop
> in the Name of Love [...]'[198]

This is reminiscent of an aforementioned earlier poem, part 10 of 'Liverpool Poems' which reads:

> Prostitutes in the snow in Canning St like strange erotic snowmen[199]

Of course, Henri is making reference to the musical girl group, led by Diana Ross, and their 1965 hit record, 'Stop in the Name of Love!'.[200] The fact that Henri mentions the singers 'standing' is clearly a reference to the movement that the group made when singing the song. One hand was located behind the body and the other hand motioned a clear 'stop' signal. The prostitutes on Broadway would, no doubt, have been looking for custom.

In 'Pennsylvania Landscape from the Air' the integration between art and poetry is again brought to the fore. There are a series of these poems that look at the landscape of America from the air and, with his painterly eye, Henri describes vivid scenes such as 'parallel brown treemossed hills' from the aforementioned 'Pennsylvania Landscape from the Air' and from 'Ohio Landscape from the Air' we are treated to 'patterns of township/clumps of red gold orange trees [...]'[201] A clear indication of the relationship to painting is 'night landscape to NYC' from the air that is dedicated 'for the American painters of the/1950s: MR/AR/BN'[202] The poem exhibits some abstract imagery, different to the other landscape pieces in the poem:

[...] sprinkled with pale yellowgreen lights

bright neon jewelry (sic)
laid out on plump blackvelvet display cushions[203]

This simile of the cityscape below the clouds being bright neon jewellery, works particularly well with the ground being likened to a 'blackvelvet' cushion. Henri takes the image and presents it in an abstract form, to mimic the work of the painters. This was a practice of writing used, at times, by Frank O'Hara, a poet of the so-called New York School of the late 1950s and early 1960s.

1972 was a busy year for Henri. Aside from publishing *America*, he became President of the Liverpool Academy of Arts, toured as 'Henri and Friends', an ensemble that included Vivien Stanshall, a member of The Bonzo Dog Doo-Dah Band and various musicians and performers. Perhaps most importantly to Henri, he won second prize at the John Moores Painting Prize. This prestigious competition was initiated in 1957 at the instigation of Liverpool businessman and founder of Littlewoods Pools, John Moores. Moores was concerned with the lack of opportunity for artists outside of London to showcase their work and argued that Liverpool's Walker Art Gallery should 'mount an exhibition of painting [...] embracing the best and most vital work being done today throughout the country'.[204] The inaugural exhibition was intended to be a one-off, but its success meant that it became a biennial event. It remains one of the most sought after prizes in British art. Previous outright prizewinners include David Hockney, Peter Doig and Lisa Milroy. Henri's prizewinning painting remains in the Walker's permanent collection.

Henri kept busy between publications. He toured both as a poet and as an artist and his work was displayed throughout the UK and Europe. In 1973, he revisited the USA and visited Canada to read his work. He worked as a visiting lecturer at Bradford Polytechnic in the Community Arts department. 1974 saw the reissue of *The Mersey Sound.* This new edition, subtitled 'Revised Edition' was later reissued in 1983 in a matching edition with 'New Volume'. The 1983 edition, with its rather typically 80s cover, features the three poets on a slipway at New Brighton, on the Wirral peninsula, with Liverpool in the hazy distance. Henri appears in the centre of the trio in a faux fur coat. In the corner of the cover, a yellow tab made to look like a sticker in a handwriting style font, declares 'Over one-quarter of a million copies sold', a phenomenal amount for a poetry anthology. The rear-cover blurb makes for interesting reading, noting that 'these are poems that echo the mood of the sixties.'[205]

1975 saw the release of *The Best of Henri,* published by Jonathan Cape. Released in a hardback version, as well as a trade paperback, the book was subtitled on the title page as 'Selected Poems 1960-1970'.[206] The book, wrapped in photographs of the author taken by his girlfriend at the time, Sue Sterne, strangely comes without blurbs. The inside fly leaf notes 'here is Henri encapsulated' and to an extent, the book does indeed capture the best of Henri at that point, with the 'bright song-like verses [which] celebrate both Romanticism and realism, the world of pale pink roses and that of pie and chips.'[207] There is a major exclusion in this selection. However, the poem 'I Want to Paint' was featured in *The Mersey Sound* and extracts from the poem regularly appear, fittingly, at Henri exhibitions. This is an important poem of Henri's, that needs further consideration.

Written in two long parts, 'I Want to Paint' is reminiscent of early Henri, with its references to popular culture and heroes, and the surreal humour that typified the work from the 1960s. 'Part One' consists of three stanzas, each beginning with a reiteration of the poem's title. Henri references his own art in the opening stanza with an allusion to 'The Death of a Bird in the City' paintings from 1961 and 1964-5:

> I want to paint
> 2000 dead birds crucified on a background of night

There is also a direct reference to the 1964 work 'The Entry of Christ Into Liverpool':

> The Entry of Christ into Liverpool in 1966[208]

The final two lines of the opening stanza make reference both to a friend and a hero while criticizing the establishment, and offer the reader the first glimpse of the surrealist tone that follows:

> The installation of Roger McGough to the Chair of Poetry at Oxford
> Francis Bacon making the President's Speech at the Royal Academy Dinner[209]

The third stanza begins with a lightly funny and cheeky image: 'I want to paint/50 life-sized nudes of Marianne Faithfull/(all of them painted from life)', and continues with references to Piccadilly in Manchester, 'A painting as big as Piccadilly full of neon signs buses'[210] Henri had painted a pair of paintings in 1962 and 1964, called 'Piccadilly Painting' and 'Piccadilly Painting II'. The area also appears in the long poem *Autobiography*, with stanza 14 of Part Three 1957-1964, referencing the paintings (the stanza is a vivid description of them):

> 14
> painting huge canvases of Piccadilly
> Guinness Clock MOTHER'S PRIDE
> bright garden   yellow flowers   grey buildings
> huge hoardings for eggs or cornflakes

DAFFODILS ARE NOT REAL
scrawled defiantly across the middle
[...] [211]

There is a useful perspective on Henri's practice at the time in the *Adrian Henri: Paintings 1953-1998* catalogue:

> Advertising came into its own somewhere about the mid-fifties and then the colour supplements came out in the early sixties. In my early Piccadilly paintings there are several transcriptions of adverts.[212]

We can see the above references to advertising with 'Guinness' and 'Mother's Pride' bread, and in 'I Want to Paint' with its neon, which was a medium favoured by advertising executives in the late 1950s and early 1960s.

'I Want to Paint' shifts focus with the third stanza of Part One. Here Henri focuses on politics, railing against the monarchy:

> I want to paint
> The assassination of the entire Royal Family
> Enormous pictures of every pavingstone in Canning Street
> The Beatles composing a new National Anthem
> Brian Patten writing poems with a flamethrower on disused
>   ferryboats[213]

Here the tone of violence, ranging from murder to flamethrowers, is tempered somewhat by the notion of The Beatles providing a new anthem. In the mid-sixties the National Anthem was still played at the end of screenings at the cinema, and also at the end of a day's broadcast on TV. Canning Street, as I have noted, is where Henri lived in the mid to late 1960s. The final stanza of Part One keeps the reader firmly located in Liverpool with references to the new Metropolitan Cathedral of Christ the King, the construction of which began in 1962 and was completed in 1967, and St George's Hall, the neo-classical building on the city's Lime

Street. The opening line alludes to the new Cathedral's modernist architecture with the surreal image of 'A new cathedral 50 miles high made entirely of pram-wheels' and the final lines neatly close the opening part:

> I want to paint
> I LOVE YOU across the steps of St George's Hall
> I want to paint
> > pictures.[214]

The opening stanza of Part Two replicates the opening stanza of Part One. It juxtaposes death and that familiar Henri image, the pink heart:

> I want to paint
> The Simultaneous and Historical Faces of Death
> 10,000 shocking pink hearts with your name on [...]

The stanza continues the love theme with lines such as 'A full-scale map of the World with YOU at the centre.'[215] The replication of theme is also in evidence with these lines from the second stanza in Part Two:

> A black-and-red flag flying over Parliament
> I want to paint
> Every car crash on all the motorways of England
> Père Ubu drunk at 11 o'clock at night in Lime Street [...][216]

The black and red flag, which incidentally appears in both the poem and painting 'The Entry of Christ Into Liverpool', is the flag of the anarchist movement; and Henri again references his own painting – this time it is 1962's 'Père Ubu in Liverpool'. The poem finishes with a list, a favoured Henri mode, of all the things that he would still like to paint, but ultimately knew he couldn't – a list demonstrating an acute political and social awareness:

I want to paint
Pictures that children can play hopscotch on
Pictures that can be used as evidence at Murder trials
Pictures that can be used to advertise cornflakes
Pictures that can be used to frighten naughty children
Pictures worth their weight in money
Pictures that tramps can live in
Pictures that children would find in their stockings on
    Christmas morning
Pictures that teenage lovers can send each other
I want to paint
            pictures [217]

We can see 'I Want to Paint' as an artistic manifesto, a statement of poetics regarding the art. But what about the poetry? In an English text book for schools *Wider Aspects of English* by D.S. Higgins, published in 1974, a fascinating chapter is entitled 'Meet Adrian Henri'.[218]

Bearing in mind that the book was aimed at secondary school children, Henri gives the readers an insight into two poems, 'Where'er You Walk' and 'Nightsong'. Both poems appeared in *The Mersey Sound* and 'Nightsong' appeared in Henri's 1968 debut collection, *Tonight at Noon*. Henri explains his technique, which is primarily updating older poems (in this case 'Where'er You Walk' is a version of a poem by Alexander Pope, whilst 'Nightsong' adapts a poem by Byron) and notes that 'I tried to put together two very different ways of writing. One is the kind of Eighteenth Century English verse that relies for its effect on "conceits" – exaggerated, elaborate ideas expressed in fanciful language.' He goes on:

My own poetry [...] is always attempting to speak with absolute simplicity, with the content, vocabulary and speech-patterns of someone living in the north of England now, and to express emotion as directly as possible.[219]

We have a firmer, more formalised notion of Henri's poetics if we return to *Tonight at Noon*. At the rear of the book, 18 pages of prose appear, entitled 'Notes on Painting and Poetry'.[220] Referring to image in poetry and art, Henri highlights his discomfort with 'The Movement' and the perceived tendency for poems by Movement poets to 'be a whole poem based on one image, rather like a weak Nescafé.'[221] Henri instead advocates poets such as Arp, Lorca or Apollinaire, who 'work in terms of successions of images.'[222] This can be seen as a way of identifying Henri's practice as distinct from the painting. Referring to 'I Want to Paint', Henri notes that the poem 'is not about painting as such at all but a catalogue of ideal images without reference to media.'[223] We can deduce from this that Henri was keen to be active in a process driven poetics. Catherine Marcangeli, in her foreword to *Adrian Henri: Total Artist*, points to T.S. Eliot's 'Tradition and the Individual Talent' as being instrumental in pioneering Henri's poetics. If we turn to Eliot and the idea of the poet/artist having an awareness of what's gone before and that no poet/artist has 'complete meaning alone', we can spot this influence in many poems of Henri's such as 'Me' which was discussed earlier.[224]

Originally a Christmas greeting, 1975's *Haiku* was printed privately for Henri by Liverpool's Anvil Press. The haiku contained in the publication would later be published in *Collected Poems*. Taking his cue from the Kerouacian or Western idea of the haiku (Kerouac called his haiku by the non-traditional plural haikus), Henri shifted away from the traditional Japanese mode of the form. Writing in *Stepping Stones: A Way into Haiku*, Martin Lucas argues that 'haiku is not a *descriptive* poetry, it is a *reflective* poetry.'[225] Lucas further mentions the important divide between Western and Japanese haiku:

Haiku is not *Haiku*. Our 'haiku' are not *haiku*. *Haiku* – here identified by italics is a very short form of Japanese verse. It would not be quite true to say that it can only be written *by* a Japanese, but it can only be written *in* Japanese, and it would require the same level of fluency in Japanese culture, history and literary tradition as in language.[226]

The major difference between the Western and the traditional haiku is the syllabic count. Traditional haiku has seventeen syllables or an *on* on a single line. In an attempt to match this in English, the seventeen syllables are usually cast over three lines in 5, 7 and 5.[227] Kerouac said this about haiku:

Above all, a haiku must be very simple and free of all poetics trickery and make a little picture and yet be as airy and graceful as a Vivaldi pastorella.[228]

The thirteen haiku contained in Henri's pamphlet follow the tradition of not titling the poems, but also follows a Henri tradition of dedicating work to people. Again, there is a problem in deciphering the differences between the original publication of *Haiku* with the version in *Collected Poems*. For example, the dedicatory statement in the pamphlet is unitalicised, whereas in the *Collected Poems* it is. With the pamphlet being unpaginated and each haiku being on its own page, the version of the text in the *Collected* appears over fussy. Similarly, a haiku that is dedicated to the poet Ted Joans, has its opening line printed in bold, whereas in the *Collected* it is not. This gives the appearance that this line in bold print is a title.

The Henri haiku clearly owe a debt to the work that the Beat writers did in promoting the notion of the Western haiku. Allen Ginsberg, Henri's old friend was also a practitioner. Gary Snyder was introduced to the haiku by fellow Bay Area poet, Kenneth Rexroth, and then proceeded to introduce the form to Kerouac and Ginsberg. Kerouac would go on to use the form throughout his writing career and integrated them into books such as *The Dharma Bums* and *Some of the Dharma*.[229] Ginsberg added a new twist to the haiku in the 1980s by creating his 'American Sentences' which were single sentences comprising seventeen syllables.

The opening haiku in Henri's pamphlet follows a traditional Henri trope by adding 'I think of you'. The full haiku, centred in the pamphlet, reads:

> leaves fall from the privet-trees in the Autumn backyard
> – I think of you[230]

In traditional Henri style, the second haiku offers a mix of domesticity and the nature of the city:

> This morning,
> throwing out last night's beer,
> I gave a party to the birds.[231]

The stronger pieces do feel like more traditional Western haiku. Take this example:

> Hillsides veiled with fern
> Foxgloves last seen with you
> A hundred miles away.[232]

This maintains the theme of love, mixed with travel and nature described specifically. This theme of nature is paramount to the notion of haiku, in particular the seasons. Henri manages to follow, to an extent, these typical 'rules'. As well as the dedications, and seasonal references, he allows for another familiar Henri notion, the city, to appear. Hardman Street, a major thoroughfare in Liverpool city centre, makes an appearance, as does the River Mersey (it is a dedicatee) and Euston Square in London. It is worth noting that the train from Liverpool terminates at London Euston station.

Henri would continue to write short poems throughout his writing career, though not as designated haiku. However, it is clear that the poems meant something to Henri as they made the leap from a small private publication to the *Collected Poems.*

Notes

[154] *The Amazing Adventures of The Liverpool Scene* (UK release: RCA Victor SF 7995; US RCA Victor LSP-4189). The album was produced by seminal DJ John Peel who called Henri 'one of the great non-singers of our time'. The album appeared in the UK in November 1968 with the US release following in 1969.

[155] The second Liverpool Scene album was released on RCA Victor Records in the UK in May 1969; Catalogue No: SF 8057.

[156] For more about The Liverpool Scene, see former member Andy Roberts' website www.andyrobertsmusic.com and also www.adrianhenri.com. Accessed 12 February 2017.

[157] Adrian Henri, 'Six Landscapes for Susan' in *Poems for Wales and Six Landscapes for Susan* (Gillingham: Arc Publications, 1970), np.

[158] Ibid.

[159] Ibid.

[160] See the details regarding his first collection of the 1970s, *Autobiography,* below.

[161] Adrian Henri, 'Poems for Wales' in *Poems for Wales and Six Landscapes for Susan*, np.

[162] 'Batpoem' in Adrian Henri *Collected Poems*, p38.

[163] Adrian Henri, 'Poems for Wales' in *Poems for Wales and Six Landscapes for Susan*, np.

[164] Catherine Marcangeli interview broadcast in *Sex, Chips and Poetry: 50 Years of The Mersey Sound* dir. by Ellen Hobson, BBC Four, first shown 1 October 2017.

[165]'Liverpool Poems' in *Collected Poems*, pp30-31.

[166]'Piccadilly Poems' in *Collected Poems*, pp6-7.

[167]'Poems for Wales' in *Poems for Wales and Six Landscapes for Susan*, np.

[168]Ibid.

[169]Adrian Henri, introduction to *Collected Poems*, np

[170]Adrian Henri, foreword to *Autobiography* (London: Jonathan Cape, 1971), np.

[171]Ibid.

[172]The dedication reads IN MEMORIAM Albert Johnson d. May 13th 1970; Frances Johnson, née Potter d. May 16th 1970; Emma Henri, née Johnson d. June 3rd, 1970; Arthur Maurice Henri d. June 29th 1970.

[173]Adrian Henri, *Autobiography*, p10.

[174]Frank Milne, *Adrian Henri: Paintings 1953-1998*, p7.

[175]See *Adrian Henri: Paintings 1953-1998*, p50.

[176]Adrian Henri, *Autobiography*, p13.

[177]Adrian Henri, *Autobiography*, p13.

[178]In the introduction to *Autobiography*, Henri points to his poetics regarding the poems in the book: 'The book covers the years 1932-64. I have made it a research project into the person I was at each stage, using old photographs, letters, notebooks and unpublished poems, from which a number of words and images were taken. The last section refers to last summer and might perhaps have been intercut with the earlier sections. I found I could not say anything fresh about my life 1964-70, possibly because it is already too well-documented in existing published work [...]' Introduction to *Autobiography*, p5. It is useful to note that Henri makes reference to a specific era, 1957-64, that the poem 'Poem for Liverpool 8' is concerned with, when Henri was settling in the area. 'Autobiography' also appears in *Collected Poems*, pp. 129-166 and in *Adrian Henri: Selected and Unpublished Poems 1965-2000*, ed, Catherine Marcangeli, (Liverpool: Liverpool

University Press, 2007), pp251-259.

[179]Adrian Henri, 'Poem for Liverpool 8' in *Autobiography*, pp31-32.

[180]Adrian Henri, 'Poem for Liverpool 8' in *Autobiography*, pp31-32.

[181]Interview by the author with Catherine Marcangeli took place on 7 July 2007, at the Mount Street home in Liverpool that she shared with Adrian Henri.

[182]Adrian Henri, 'Poem for Liverpool 8' in *Autobiography*, p31. Henri misspells Catharine Street in both *Autobiography* and *Collected Poems*.

[183]Ibid.

[184]Ibid.

[185]Adrian Henri, 'Poem for Liverpool 8' in *Autobiography*, p32.

[186]The cemetery was in the disused quarry immediately below and behind the Cathedral. Henri is making reference to when the cemetery was tidied up and gardens laid out in the space. Many of the gravestones line the walk through the small tunnel leading to the gardens. However, the space has recently been reclaimed and has its own website http://stjamescemetery.org. Many of Liverpool's elder statesmen and famous sons and daughters, such as William Huskisson, Kitty Wilkinson and William Brown are buried in the cemetery.

[187]Adrian Henri, 'Poem for Liverpool 8' in *Autobiography*, p32.

[188]Ibid, pp31-32.

[189]Adrian Henri, 'Poem for Summer 1967' in *Autobiography*, pp39-40.

[190]Adrian Henri, 'Poem for Summer 1967' in *Autobiography*, p39.

[191]Ibid, p40.

[192]William Carlos Williams, introduction to *The Wedge* in *Selected Essays of William Carlos Williams* (New York: New Directions, 1969), p256.

[193]Adrian Henri, 'A City of Poems', in Robinson, ed. *Liverpool Accents: Seven Poets and a City*, pp35-38. Henri's book *City* uses the image of an *A-Z* map with the word 'City' marked in red. This is possibly a

reference to Charles Olson's *Maximus Poems* (New York: Jargon/ Corinth, 1975) that has a map of the area of Gloucester, Massachusetts on its cover.

[194]Adrian Henri, 'Untitled' in *America* in *Collected Poems*, p123.

[195]'Mrs Albion, You've Got a Lovely Daughter' in *The Mersey Sound*, p5; David Bateman, 'Adrian Henri: Singer of Meat and Flowers' in Wade, ed. *Gladsongs and Gatherings*, p91.

[196]Adrian Henri, *America* in *Collected Poems*, p121.

[197]'14.XI.69' in *America* in *Collected Poems*, p121.

[198]'13.XI.69' in *Collected Poems*, p121.

[199]Adrian Henri, 'Liverpool Poems' in *Collected Poems*, p31.

[200]The song reached number 1 in America and number 7 in the UK.

[201]'Ohio Landscape from the Air' in *America* in *Collected Poems*, p124.

[202]These painters, Mark Rothko, Ad Reinhardt and Barnett Newman, were part of the Abstract Expressionist movement that also included the likes of Jackson Pollock, Elaine De Kooning and Willem De Kooning.

[203]'Ohio Landscape from the Air' in *America* in *Collected Poems*, p124.

[204]John Moores from the 1957 exhibition catalogue. For more about the John Moores Prize, see http://www.liverpoolmuseums.org.uk/walker/ johnmoores/

[205]Adrian Henri, Roger McGough and Brian Patten, *The Mersey Sound Revised Edition* (London: Penguin Books, 1983). The full rear cover blurb reads: 'Irreverent, Sardonic, Funny and Sad, these are the poems that echo the mood of the Sixties. *The Mersey Sound* is a selection of the early work of three of our best-known poets. Adrian Henri, Roger McGough and Brian Patten were part of the "pop poetry" movement of the sixties. Innovative in both form and style, they revolutionized the traditional boundaries of the genre, bringing poetry down from the dusty shelf and onto the street. *The Mersey Sound,* originally published in 1967, has become one of the most popular poetry anthologies, selling over a million copies. For this revised edition new poems have

been added, whilst some originally included have been reworked.'

[206]Adrian Henri, *The Best of Henri* (London: Jonathan Cape, 1975).

[207]Flyleaf to *The Best of Henri*. The pale pink rose is a mistake here. Henri was, and is, still known for the pale pink love heart.

[208]'I Want to Paint' in *The Mersey Sound*, p14.

[209]Ibid.

[210]Ibid.

[211]*Autobiography*, p37. The poem also appears in *Collected Poems*, p155.

[212]Adrian Henri in *Adrian Henri: Paintings 1953-1998*, p56.

[213]'I Want to Paint' in *The Mersey Sound*, p14.

[214]'I Want to Paint' in *The Mersey Sound*, p15.

[215]'I Want to Paint' in *The Mersey Sound*, p14.

[216]Ibid, p15.

[217]'I Want to Paint' in *The Mersey Sound*, pp15-16.

[218]'Meet Adrian Henri' in D.S. Higgins, *Wider Aspects of English* (London: Cassell, 1974), pp26-31.

[219] Ibid, pp28-29.

[220]'Notes on Painting and Poetry' in *Tonight at Noon*, pp63-81. This was later usefully republished in *Adrian Henri: Total Artist*, ed. Catherine Marcangeli (London: Occasional Papers, 2014).

[221]Adrian Henri, 'Notes on Painting and Poetry' in Marcangeli, ed. *Adrian Henri: Total Artist*, p114. Poetry associated with the Movement, which was prominent in the late 1950s and beyond, include the work of Philip Larkin, Elizabeth Jennings, Donald Davie and Thom Gunn.

[222]Ibid.

[223]Adrian Henri, 'Notes on Painting and Poetry' in Marcangeli, ed. *Adrian Henri: Total Artist*, p114.

[224]T.S. Eliot, 'Tradition and Individual Talent', *The Egoist*, No 4, Vol VI, (1919), pp54-55.

[225]Martin Lucas, *Stepping Stones: A Way into Haiku* (Ramsgate: The British Haiku Society, 2007), p7.

[226]Ibid, p5.

[227]For more about the notion of Kerouacian haiku(s) see Regina Weinreich's introduction to Jack Kerouac, *Book of Haikus* (London: Enitharmon, 2004). The book, edited by Weinreich, contains a wide range of Kerouac's haiku(s) beginning with the manuscript folder titled 'Book of Haikus' to 1966's 'Northport Haikus'. The material is sourced from letters, published and unpublished, unpublished material and Kerouac's own books.

[228]Rear cover of Jack Kerouac, *Book of Haikus*.

[229]Jack Kerouac, *The Dharma Bums* (London: Penguin Books, 2000) and *Some of the Dharma* (New York: Penguin, 1999).

[230]Adrian Henri, *Haiku* (Liverpool: Privately printed, 1975), np.

[231]Adrian Henri, 'Haiku' in *Collected Poems*, p166. I shall use the *Collected Poems* as the source, as 'Haiku' in its pamphlet form was a strict limited edition.

[232]Ibid, p167.

3

ART & POETRY, POETRY & ART

One Year (1976), *City Hedges* (1977), *From the Loveless Motel* (1980), *Penny Arcade* (1983) and *New Volume* (1983; Henri, McGough and Patten)

AS HENRI'S ART PRACTICE CONTINUED IN the 1970s, with a level of success that saw him become president of the Liverpool Academy of Arts, win second prize at the prestigious John Moores Painting Prize and exhibit widely around the UK, it is understandable that poetry took a slightly lesser role in his wider creative practice.[233] Henri's reputation as an artist was further enhanced by the publication of *Environments and Happenings* in 1974.[234] This book title was appropriated for the title of a major exhibition as part of the Liverpool Biennial at John Moores University in 2014, and later at the ICA in London, in 2015. For the American market the book was titled *Total Art: Environments and Happenings* and was instrumental in signposting the importance of Liverpool, and particularly Henri, in establishing the important crossover between poetry and art in the UK. Henri says of the Happenings that occurred first in the city:

> The first happenings in England were done by a group of artists and poets in Liverpool in 1962, as a result of my reading an article by Allan Kaprow earlier that year. I had been making assemblages, and

as with Kaprow, happenings seemed a natural extension. The happenings were presented as part of a Merseyside Arts Festival in 1962 and 1963, along with poetry-and-music and folk-evenings. The 'events', as we called them, quickly became a popular form of entertainment: a mixture of poetry, rock'n'roll and assemblage. Later events had live music by local 'Merseybeat' groups, for instance the Roadrunners and the Clayton Squares, as in *Nightblues,* 1963.[235]

This highlights the collaborative nature of Henri's practice that places him at the forefront of the counter culture of British art and poetry of the 1960s.

The mid 1970s saw the publication of retrospective publications that kept Henri's poetry profile high. In 1973 the revised edition of *The Mersey Sound* was published by Penguin. This edition was expanded to 152 pages, from the original 1967 page count of 128. (The later 1983 revised edition would increase the page count to 157.)[236] *The Best of Henri,* a selected poems covering the years 1960-1970, was published by Jonathan Cape in 1975. The book was dedicated to Joyce Henri (his former wife) and Susan Sterne, a girlfriend who took the book's cover photographs of Henri. *The Best of Henri* was called 'disappointing' by Phil Bowen, who argues that it was something of a 'filler. *Out-takes* would have been more appropriate.'[237] This seems unfair. The book may have been a stop-gap collection, but all of the 'greatest hits' of Henri's poetry career to-date were included. Poems such as 'Me', 'The Entry of Christ Into Liverpool' and 'Love Poem' make an appearance, alongside the long poem 'City', an important part of Henri's oeuvre, which closes the book.

Following a similar path to *Haiku* and *Poems for Wales and Six Landscapes for Susan,* Arc Publications published the pamphlet-length poem 'One Year' in 1976.[238] Subtitled '*1973-74/Liverpool – Totleigh Barton – /Hollywood – New York City-/Much Wenlock*', the poem traces the poet's movements with a certain sense of linearity. The third stanza, located in Liverpool, could have appeared in a poem from the late 1960s. Again, daffodils appear alongside 'concrete promenades', reminiscent of 'Albion's most lovely daughter sat on the banks of the Mersey/dangling her landing stage in the water', the opening line of 'Mrs Albion, You've got a Lovely Daughter'.[239] 'One Year' is important as it draws on Henri's poetics of memory in poems such as 'Autobiography' and 'City' yet somehow confirms the poetic shift that appears in the following full collection, *City Hedges*. There is a shift towards the lyrical and pastoral that matches the shift in Henri's art practice. This shift of perspective, away from the city and towards the pastoral can be in part explained by the travels he made during this time and the fact that Henri had suffered heart attacks and was in a more reflective frame of mind.

Henri was first invited to tutor at the Arvon Foundation in Totleigh Barton in Devon during 1973. He became a regular tutor at the Foundation. The courses at Arvon offer writers residential programmes and retreats in three countryside locations.[240] This shift towards the pastoral can be further traced to after Henri pocketed his £2,000 prize money from the John Moores Painting Prize. He was invited to spend the summer in Much Wenlock in Shropshire. Henri later commented that this was a turning point in his artistic practice:

> What I found [in Much Wenlock] was a deep hedge along a disused railway cutting. This very ordinary bit of English hedgerow has occupied my time ever since. I've tried to make the painting as botanically accurate as possible [and in many cases they are] carried on laterally on another canvas.[241]

This experience of spending time in rural parts of Britain, as well as being based in Liverpool and visiting the metropolises of

New York and Los Angeles, clearly had an effect on Henri's poetry, as evidenced by the title of his next full collection.

City Hedges: Poems 1972-1976 was published by Jonathan Cape in 1977. The first full collection of work published since *Autobiography* in 1971, it begins strongly with the poem 'Morning Song'. This poem sets the tone for the collection. It begins with a telling opening two lines (later repeated for good measure in the final stanza). It is worth bearing in mind Henri's prize-winning painting in the John Moores Painting Prize was from a series called 'Meat Paintings'. The song element of the poem's title is re-emphasised with the repetition of the opening stanza:

> *Of meat and flowers I sing*
> *Butchers and gardeners:*
> *Songs thrown bleeding onto counters*
> *Reaching up to the sun through city backyards.*[242]

Again, we find the familiar Henri image of the city meeting nature. This is a serious book, its themes matching the funereal tone of parts of *Autobiography*. There are poems titled 'Wartime', 'The Dance of Death' and 'The Triumph of Death'. Perhaps the centrepiece of the collection is the poem dedicated to David Gascoyne, 'Metropolis'. Gascoyne was a leading Surrealist poet who lived in Paris before the Second World War and became associated with the likes of Max Ernst, André Breton and Salvador Dali. He translated many Surrealist works into English, making them accessible to a British readership. 'Metropolis' has its themes located in the transition of the natural world into an ordered sense of the metropolitan. The opening of the four numbered stanzas immediately sets the scene, partially by being split into two unnumbered parts and through the use of contrasting imagery of the natural and the manmade:

gravelponds along long lines
fruit-trees heavy in the autumn sunlight
disturbed only by the falling brickdust
and the distant roar of engines in the morning air.[243]

The alliterative opening line alludes to travel, perhaps by train (Henri didn't drive and used public transport) and there is a sense of calmness disturbed by man's intrusion. This is further shown later in the first stanza with 'squashed hedgehogs dying owls rabbits screaming' [...]/before the march of giant earthmovers.'[244] The poem continues in this vein, pitting the battle of the natural against the march of so-called progress. Perhaps most telling is the use of technological imagery. We need to remember that this is a poem of the 1970s, when technology such as computers and videotape were in their infancy. There is an ecological awareness within the poem that is particularly powerful:

stagnant pools rainbowed with oil
where fishes once swarmed[245]

The imposition by the human on the natural world and the associated consequences, was a theme which Henri would return to in his poetry throughout his career. A sense of the past is foregrounded in the final stanza where 'silver trains swish and rattle into blackness' and 'old videotapes of trees played rushingly past the empty/windows/stereo birdsong through the airconditioned silence.' This eco-critical stance perhaps was influenced by Gary Snyder, a poet whose work Henri was certainly familiar with, through the influence of the Beat Generation poets on his work.

Another 'song' to match those of 'Morning Song', 'Evening Song', 'Citysong', 'Dreamsong' and 'Two Lullabys' is 'A Song for A.E. Housman'. This poem is noticeable for its rigid form. Henri opts for a strict A, B, A, B rhyme scheme and strong assertive rhythm in ballad stanzas. This is shown by the second stanza:

> In Wenlock Town the drink goes down
> The laughter flows like wine
> In Wenlock Town the leaves are brown
> And you are no longer mine [246]

There is a sense of melancholy that permeates throughout the poem, similar to earlier poems such as 'Adrian Henri's Talking After Christmas Blues' and 'Without You', which works against the quickfire metre. Henri was not usually known for his use of traditional form and 'A Song for A.E. Housman' stands out due to its formal construction, echoing Housman's strong formal sense as well as concentrating on loco-specificity of Housman's most famous poems in *A Shropshire Lad*.[247]

A poem that would have appeared more familiar to readers of Henri is 'Three Landscapes'. Building on *Poems for Wales and Six Landscapes for Susan*, the three short numbered parts would, at least structurally, feel at home in any previous Henri publication:

> red earth
> stillness
> lane shuttered
> high
> above
> the sound of ash trees.[248]

Again, nature is the subject. The lane is 'shuttered', perhaps by the high hedgerows that Henri found so inspiring during his trip to Much Wenlock.

As with any Adrian Henri collection of poetry, love makes an appearance. One of the more successful poems is 'Butterfly' dedicated to Carol Ann Duffy. Henri had met Duffy previously while touring with the band Grimms (the post-Liverpool Scene band comprising Henri, Roger McGough, John Gorman, Neil Innes, Mike McGear, Brian Patten and Andy Roberts) and she later came to Liverpool to study philosophy at Liverpool University. Henri and Duffy became lovers and the tenderness of the early days of their relationship is in evidence in the poem 'Butterfly':

Sing
of your gift
for your lover
as I fall
flicker against your feet[249]

Again, there is natural imagery peppered throughout the poem. Aside from the title, there is 'evening sunlight' and a 'tiny rainbow'.

The only one of the original three *Mersey Sound* poets remaining in Liverpool, (though McGough had briefly returned to the city in the mid-1970s), Henri busied himself with readings and events. Casting himself in the role of organiscr again, he returned to the scene of the original Happenings, the former Hope Hall, by now known as the Everyman Theatre. With funding for a reading series, perhaps aided by his role as President of the Merseyside Arts Association, the series was titled 'Henri's Hope Street Poets' (Hope Street being the road where the Everyman is located). The series of formal readings featured local poets and guests such as David Gascoyne, Christopher Logue and W.S. Graham. In January 1979 Henri visited Paris to read with fellow poets James Simmons, Edwin Morgan, Paul Buck, Kenneth White and Andrew Motion, under the banner 'British Poets for Arc'. The event held at the prestigious Musée d'Art Moderne de La Ville de Paris goes someway in highlighting the success that Henri had enjoyed post *The Mersey Sound.*[250]

Henri's next collection, *From the Loveless Motel: Poems 1976-1979*, again published by Jonathan Cape, appeared in 1980. There

is a clear pattern forming with the subtitling of each collection
locating the years in which the poetry was written: a sense of diaristic
autobiography was becoming a familiar trait. The book opens with
a poem on familiar Henri ground, with the interruption of nature
by man.

'Death in the Suburbs' comes with a preface: 'The end of the
world will surely come/in Bromley South or Orpington'. This image
of forgotten places, would later be echoed by Morrissey in his song
'Everyday is Like Sunday' with the lyric 'This is the coastal town/
that they forgot to close down/come Armageddon come.'[251] Henri's
opening stanza provides us with a scene of domestic bliss, as typified
by suburban life: the 'villas detached and undetached/islanded with
flowering cherry' and 'each man's garden a province unto itself/
linked only by birdsong'.[252] This domesticity and portrait of
suburban life is shattered at the beginning of the second stanza:

> the earth
> moves
> sudden
> tiny snowstorms of cherryblossom
> a black cat runs apprehensive [253]

The image of the earth moving gives way to the sense that
something is happening to break the slumber of suburbia. The
black cat, often seen as a symbol in British culture of good luck, is
running scared. This apprehension is reiterated in the following
stanza with 'deepfreezes burst open/prepackaged meals spilling
everywhere/invitations to whist-drives coffee-mornings/letters to
long-haired sons at campus universities/never to be delivered.' [254]
This foreboding tone continues throughout the poem until the
final stanza clarifies that a lone picnicker on the beach is witness to
a nuclear attack, and 'see(s) the horizon catch fire'.[255] But the
continued references to normality, 'the last slice of ham a packet of

biscuits the small black/notebook/slip away unseen', reverts the reader's attention to the earlier calm of the suburbs. The final lines of the poem confirm the destructive force of something all consuming: 'one drifting pink petal/catches the dying sunlight.'[256] The finality of the failing sunlight, it is dying, hints at something larger than dusk.

At the heart of the book is the title poem of the collection, dedicated in memoriam to Elvis Presley. Presley had died in August 1977 of a heart attack and his legacy was still keenly felt by his fans. The poem is subtitled 'A lovepoem for America'. As we know, Henri had a strong affinity with the United States, through his connection to Ginsberg, Creeley, the Beats and the New York School poets, having toured there with the poetry/rock band The Liverpool Scene in the 1960s and early 1970s and having published his long poem 'America' in 1972. This affinity would continue and be in evidence in the last two collections of poetry to be published in his lifetime.

'From the Loveless Motel' is suggestive of early long poems of Henri's such as 'The Entry of Christ into Liverpool'. There are repeated motifs and refrains reminiscent of the techniques used in the earlier long poems. 'From the Loveless Motel' features the refrains 'WALK DON'T WALK' and 'YIELD', alongside other instructions and signs such as 'THE WORLD'S MOST UNUSUAL DRUGSTORE' and 'EXIT THROUGH THE DOORS WITH THE FLASHING SYMBOLS'.[257] Perhaps the most recognisable Henri trait appears early in the poem's New York section:

WALK DON'T WALK

giant puffs of smoke from a huge cigarette
against the sky
                masks
Hallow'een masks everywhere

GENUINE IMPORTED JUNK $4[258]

This locates the reader in the hustle and bustle of Times Square in Manhattan, a place Henri would return to in his poetry and art in the future. The neon and the cigarette smoke blowing seems likely to refer to an advertisement for Camel cigarettes on the corner of 44th Street and Broadway, which was in situ from 1941 until 1967.[259]

Henri uses the image of masks in both the poem and painting titled 'The Entry of Christ into Liverpool' and in his later painting 'The Day of the Dead on Hope Street' and the wider series of paintings and drawings locating The Day of the Dead in Liverpool. Masks and Hallowe'en appear later in 'From the Loveless Motel' as Henri takes the reader across America:

> masks
> orange white Hallowe'en
> saguaros   savannas
> red deserts
> mapleleaves through mist[260]

The repeating motifs, both in the poem and in Henri's previous work, highlights his confidence in them and reiterates the modes that he is highlighting such as cultural signifiers of advertisements and masks.

Another important poem in *From the Loveless Motel* is 'Wasteland'. Here we can see the importance of the influence of T.S. Eliot on Henri's work. The poem uses direct quotes (as well as taking its title) from Eliot's 'The Waste Land', as is evident in the introduction to stanzas three and four:

> Cruellest Month
>
> We make plans to go away for Easter [...] [261]

Of course April is the month that Easter usually falls in with its attendant Bank Holidays of Good Friday and Easter Monday; and the 'cruellest month' in the Eliot text, where it is evoked as an anti-reverdie.[262] A strong theme of Henri's, as with both Eliot and Baudelaire before him, is the struggle of the natural world amongst the evolving and ever present city and general sense of modernity: the bird in the city, dead unnoticed; 'blood running merged with the neonsigns in a puddle';[263] 'the daffodils trodden underfoot';[264] and 'excited feet crushing the geraniums in St Luke's Gardens'.[265]

The final section of 'Wasteland', dedicated to André Breton, uses both sides of the page in dual columns. Here we can see Henri mixing two influences, or probably more accurately, heroes, in the shape of Breton and Eliot. This matches the modes of 'The Entry of Christ into Liverpool' and 'The Day of the Dead on Hope Street' where friends and heroes from popular and high culture intermingle.

Perhaps unsurprisingly, considering Henri's combined practice of poet and artist and his travels around the UK and USA, the ephemeral nature of a list poem appears in the collection in the form of 'Notes for an Autumn Painting'.[266] Henri considered himself a notebook poet and it was inevitable that this form would appear in his work at some point.

Henri had been made a visiting lecturer in Fine Art at Leeds Polytechnic in 1980. This was among his many artistic related activities, such as curating and being an external examiner at different art schools, and art was again being brought to the fore in his poetry too. The poem consists of 14 stanzas ranging in length from one word to three lines. As you would expect from its title, it is full of colour and these signifiers of autumn appear across the first three stanzas:

mist.

crisp leaves against grass.

pale sunrise.[267]

Again, in a throwback to earlier poems, the poem finishes with stanzas reminiscent of 'Me', a poem that featured in both Henri's debut collection and *The Mersey Sound*:

in the foreground
grass yellowed almost to whiteness

and
a space where

the person who will no longer be in the picture
should be.[268]

Using the layout to emphasise the importance of these last lines (the previous stanzas are punctuated and short), which allude to a lost relationship, Henri repeats his familiar poetic trick of writing a poem about something other than what it appears to be about.

Henri's relationship with Carol Ann Duffy had ended towards the end of the 1970s. Phil Bowen points to the failing of the relationship Henri had had prior to Duffy, with Frances Hambidge, as the inspiration for the poem 'Autumn Leaving', which is clearly a sister poem to 'Notes for an Autumn Painting'.[269] The relationship with Hambidge was long over by the time Duffy and Henri had ended their relationship, though there had been a crossover at one point. The poems of lost love in *From the Loveless Motel* are probably concerned with the break up between Duffy and Henri, though Duffy was not to move out of Henri's Mount Street home until 1983. The evidence is in the poem 'Autumn Leaving' with the lines that hark back to an earlier love poem dedicated to Duffy,

'Butterfly' and the reference to writing poetry: 'Pressing the wings of butterflies for paper/I write you poems at midnight.'[270]

'Autumn Leaving' is an interesting poem. Again, it mixes nature with the urban but with the added context of poetic practice thrown into the mix: 'dead leaves/drift through your words/cold winds/blow between sentences/eddy between paragraphs'.[271] There is also humour mixed with regret:

> At summit conferences
> we argue
> about custody of the deodorant
> and visiting hours for the cat
> at weekends.[272]

The idea of mediation taking place, with deodorant under discussion rather than children, as is usual, combined with arrangements for visitations with the cat, mocks the notion of the process of the negotiation.

In 1980 Henri began a two-year post as writer-in-residence at The Tattenhall Centre in Cheshire, funded by the then Arts Council of Great Britain. The early 1980s saw riots across the UK. In Liverpool riots began on 5 July 1981, after the arrest of a local black man, Leroy Cooper. The riots were named by the media as the 'Toxteth' riots, though the area is known locally as Liverpool 8 or L8. In his poem 'Seaport', Robert Hampson explores some of the causes of the riots.[273] In 2011, under the 30 year rule when government papers are released, it came to light that the Conservative government had urged the Prime Minister, Margaret Thatcher, to 'let Liverpool decline' and blamed the city for its own downfall after the riots.[274] The riots, which spread to other major cities such as Bristol, Birmingham, Leeds and Brixton in London, were primarily due to increasingly high unemployment and racial tensions. These events would provide Henri with material for some of his poems throughout the 1980s.

On 2 October 1982 William S. Burroughs came to Liverpool to do a signing and reading. Burroughs was in the UK to promote 'A William Burroughs Reader', published in September of 1982 by Picador books. Henri attended both the signing in Atticus Bookshop on Hardman Street and the reading later that night at a hotel in Mount Pleasant, reading his own poetry in support.[275] Also reading that night were poets Jeff Nuttall and Geoff Ward, alongside Burroughs' poet friend from New York, John Giorno. Ward was one of the organisers of the event. He was a lecturer at the University of Liverpool at the time, and had been contacted by Jon Savage, a writer and journalist, to check the viability of organising a reading in the north of England. Burroughs was booked to read in London and as long as it proved to be financially viable, was prepared to venture north. A date was booked at the Haçienda club in Manchester on 4 October and Ward managed to book the hotel and arrange the signing at Atticus. He remembers the fee being £1,000 and booked the hotel primarily as:

> It was cheap, quite neutral and had no association with any particular clientele (the finals of Miss Caribbean Liverpool were held there just before WSB's visit) but most important of all its main conference area had a huge sliding partition door. If we bombed on the night and the audience was small we could close the door to make an intimate setting, and if we filled the hall on the night there would be room.[276]

There was an audience of over a hundred at the event, and Ward remembers there being a keen reverence for Burroughs, noting that it 'may have been the only silent room with over a hundred people in it that I ever encountered in Liverpool.' Whilst remembering also that 'the Brits read politely and were politely received. I think we were all thrown a bit off our stroke by The Presence [of Burroughs].[277]

Henri's next collection, *Penny Arcade*, was published by Cape in 1983. The book was subtitled *Poems 1980-1983*, and arrived with its cover in the familiar Cape house style and a photograph of Henri reflected through the window of an amusement arcade. It continues the travel and love theme of *From the Loveless Motel* yet feels a more considered collection than the previous book. This is partly due to the range of poems on offer, alongside the familiarity of themes, and strong work such as 'Adrian Henri's Talking Toxteth Blues', and 'Rainbow'. While Phil Bowen argues that it is 'his best collection since *Autobiography*' that statement does little to acknowledge the strong work in the previous collections.[278] It also does not take into account Henri's practice of releasing pamphlets. Ambit published 'Harbour' from *Penny Arcade* as a six-page pamphlet in 1983 with drawings by Henri.

In 1983 Penguin also released the *New Volume* follow up to *The Mersey Sound*. The blurb of the book, acknowledging the influence of the original volume, points to a 'more mature, more sensitive perspective', while adding that the anthology is 'from three of the most popular contemporary poets' and that '*New Volume* is as direct, provocative and humorous as its predecessor.'[279] The cover of the book features the three poets appearing somewhat reflective, with Henri looking almost like his old friend Ginsberg, with a neatly trimmed beard and metal framed glasses.

Henri's selection consisted of 25 poems, of which 11 were taken from *From the Loveless Motel*. It opens with 'Death in the Suburbs', highlighting the importance the poet placed on this particular poem. Similarly, 'Butterfly' dedicated to Carol Ann Duffy, makes an appearance. There is an overall reflective tone running through this anthology. Of course, all three poets are older, and most of the poems by McGough and Patten are taken from a wide range of books. Patten's selections date from 1969 to 1981, while McGough uses material published between 1971 and 1982. Henri was clearly saving material for his forthcoming collection, *Penny Arcade*. As with the previous editions of *The Mersey Sound*, Henri's work features prominently and carries the most weight, in terms of number of poems published.

In correspondence between Henri and Robin Robertson at Penguin in 1982 there was a suggestion to reissue the original *The Mersey Sound* and the new volume as *Liverpool Poets I* and *Liverpool Poets II*. Henri even did a sketch of the proposed cover design.[280] He had earlier that year written to McGough with the idea of a two-volume set of *The Mersey Sound: Volume I, 1960-1970* and *The Mersey Sound: Volume II, 1970-1980*, and Henri seems to have been particularly active with the preparations of *New Volume.*[281] There are notes, in Henri's writing, housed in the Liverpool Poets Archive at the University of Liverpool, which consider presenting the three poets' work thematically, such as 'Childhood', 'Meat', 'Bomb', 'Nature' and 'City', though this did not transpire.[282]

Penny Arcade opens with 'I Have Woken This Year', with the familiar Henri themes of travel, nature and love. The poem reads like a diary entry of places visited. It is easy to ascertain the year of the poem's composition due to the lines: 'And I have woken to my fiftieth year/two thousand, two hundred and something mornings/my fiftieth year to heaven'.[283] Among the numerous places listed in the poem are Devon, Berlin, Cambridge, Würzburg, Munich, Rotterdam and the river Thames, further evidence of his travels and recollections. Liverpool, of course, is one of the places that Henri woke up in in 1982. The poem neatly shifts after 'my fiftieth year to heaven'. The tone alters, becoming more reflective though not necessarily melancholic. It almost feels as though the poem could be a part of the long poem *Autobiography:*

> ... fifty years
> and moved across the river
> one cobbled hillside exchanged
> for another cobbled hillside.[284]

The cobbled hillside 'across the river' refers to Mount Street, the home that Henri bought in the late 1960s. Clearly the location of the house was important, as Mount Street runs between Hope Street and Pilgrim Street, and was central for the College of Art and the local pubs still frequented by the College of Art crowd. Mount Street was to be Henri's home until his death. Whether it is merely reflective of the fact that Liverpool is a busy city or it is a reference to the 'Toxteth' riots, early in the book the third line of the first long stanza contrasts the sound of the police with the countryside:

> '[...] to the echoing police sirens of this city
> in the innocent white light
> of the Cheshire countryside.[285]

The final stanza adds an air of melancholy as the narratorial voice states: 'I have woken to all these years/all these places,/woken to so many worlds,/how many more summer mornings?'[286] It is a bold question in a strong opening poem. The use of a season, summer, arguably the most preferred of the seasons for Henri, is in stark contrast to the autumnal feel of much of the work in *From the Loveless Motel.*

The second poem of the collection, again a long piece, neatly continues the theme of 'I Have Woken This Year'. 'As if in a Dream' not only puns on the title of the previous poem, but delivers an early introduction to a favoured Henri subject and motif, flowers.

The poem is prefaced by an extract from the 11th-century poem by Bilhana Kavi, 'Black Marigolds'. The translation by E. Powys Mathers reads: 'Then would my love for her be ropes of flowers, and night/a black-haired lover on the breasts of day.'[287]

Interestingly, early in the poem, clearly another love poem, Henri makes another reference to the riots: 'a metallic buzzing' in the form of a trapped bluebottle that 'circles far above the city streets,/ the shattered windows.'[288] Perhaps Henri was anticipating the use of police helicopters to combat civil unrest later in that decade, or merely was observing the damage that was caused during the riots. The dream-like narrative aspects of 'As if in a Dream' appear almost as a reminder of the poem's title, particularly in the seventh stanza:

> Silver-pink horizon
> rocks imitate sheep. Sheep
> imitate rocks. Bushes
> huddle like pensioners
> round sodden bowling-greens.[289]

It is easy to see the links between the two opening poems of this collection. Places again feature prominently: London, Birmingham, Cheshire, Devon and Liverpool. The poem, 27 stanzas long, is punctuated by references to the black marigolds of the preface. Allusions to writing appear in the ninth stanza with 'I press summer words for you/into notebooks, like flowers' for them to be found 'again/faded as winter.'[290] The passing of the seasons also suggests the passing of love: the summer flowers/words that were fresh and alive, are pale and dry by winter. Catherine Marcangeli points to this motif noting, 'Adrian often used the seasons to mirror the evolution of a love story.'[291] The longest stanza of the poem, stanza ten, is preceded by '*black marigolds of summer*' and paints a picture of domesticity with an intimate lover's scene replete with 'bodysmell beneath the bedclothes, rich,/elusive as fir trees. The ghosts of loves past [...]'[292] The festive metaphor is realised with '[...] lovers yet to come, line the mantelpiece,/persistent as Christmas cards.'[293]

This strong opening to the book continues with 'Harbour'. As noted above, the poem was issued as a pamphlet by Ambit in 1983. Another lengthy poem in four numbered stanzas, clearly it was important to the author. A typically protracted love poem, it features illustrations from the author. Henri uses personification and rhyme throughout the poem, and there are obvious nautical themes and personification related to the title. This combination is highlighted by the second stanza of part one:

> the little boatlights
> harbour of your arms
> the darkness of your eyes
> reflect the bobbing sea
> folded to ourselves far
> above the rain   the quayside
> constant[294]

The harbour motif runs through the poem and is repeated throughout, alongside images of six swans, a rainbow, the stars and the sea. This repetition prepares the reader for the poem's finale, where one word lines slow the pace and conclude the poem with a slower pace:

> rain
>
> rainbow
>
> swans
>
> constant
>
> dark
>
> harbour[295]

'Rainbow' continues the natural theme of the collection (and, of course, concentrates on a rainbow, as did 'Harbour') and consists of seven stanzas dedicated to the painter Maurice Cockrill. Cockrill lived in Liverpool from 1962 until 1982, before moving to London. He was a Royal Academician and acquainted with Henri throughout his time in Liverpool. Cockrill was studying at Wrexham College of Art in North Wales and was a regular visitor to Liverpool. He was introduced to Henri in The Philharmonic pub on Hope Street and recalls that Henri was 'Mister Art' and a 'useful person to know.'[296] The poem comprises study-like sections, poetry equivalents to an artist's preparatory sketches. These vignettes are similar to Jack Kerouac's posthumously published works contained in *Book of Sketches*.[297] All of the Henri poems are located in England aside from number 6, which is located in Paris. As one would expect, there are plenty of references to colour, the seasons and allusions to aspects of painting.

If we look at '1' we can see that this immediately feels like a Henri poem. The second part is worth quoting in full: 'Now trees against the sunset, and deer/deep in wet grass and bluebells./The red mud stiff beneath our feet.'[298] This part of the poem is located in Lyndhurst, Hampshire. We can see the familiar natural world with the intrusion of the human. The sense of a couple being there, the 'our feet' is the only hint of the human in the whole piece.

'3' offers us a familiar Henri motif – daffodils (whether real or plastic as in the early poems, is unclear), which 'flood the walls/and a sweet-voiced girl wears the station sunlight in her hair.'[299] The poem is subtitled as 'York'. This is a walled city whose many civic buildings, including the station, are made of the local York stone, which is yellowish in hue. The central image then, is well made, that of sunlight and yellow and the golden glow of the girl's hair.

The Parisian section of the poem is more formal, consisting of three stanzas of 3, 2 and 2 lines. Of course, Paris with its associations of art and artists, may stand out amongst the English shires such as Cheshire and Hampshire, yet somehow feels appropriate, with its history of artists settling there. The poem, numbered '6', begins in French: '*Fête champêtre*', country fair. The remainder of the opening line is playful: 'ducks in the dusk'[300] gives little away aside from its painterly associations: 'painted butterflies over painted trees darken to autumn', sketch-like and appropriate to the general theme of the poem.[301]

Henri returns the reader to Liverpool in the poem 'Adrian Henri's Talking Toxteth Blues'. This is reminiscent, in form, of earlier poems such as 'Car Crash Blues *or* Old Adrian Henri's Interminable Talking Surrealistic Blues'[302] and 'Adrian Henri's Talking after Christmas Blues',[303] with its long lines, musical references and layout.

The Toxteth riots of 1981 had a massive impact on the city. Henri, living in Mount Street in the L1 area of the city, next to the L8 area, was at the edge of the rioting that broke out on Upper Parliament Street. Adopting a regular rhythm and rhyme, in the form of an A, A, B, B scheme, 'Adrian Henri's Talking Toxteth Blues' breaks away from its strict rhythm and rhyme by offering a coda, rather like the blues of the title. The poem also utilises layout and ellipses to highlight the differences between each of the sections within each stanza. As one would expect in a poem about rioting, there are images of broken glass, the police and general civil unrest: 'The sirens and the shouting and the TV lights,/Banging on the riotshields, petrol bombs in flames, [...]'[304] Though serious in subject matter, Henri allows humour to creep in. The second stanza's coda reads:

> Felt sick to my stomach
> ... don't cry for me ...
> ... Upper Parly.[305]

The cultural reference to 'Don't Cry for Me Argentina' from the musical *Evita* grounds itself with the mention of Upper Parly, a local abbreviation for Upper Parliament Street in Liverpool, which was at the centre of the riots. Further local dialect references include 'a busy' and 'scuffer', both colloquial references to police officers. The final coda refers to the

> ... Toxteth nightmare ...
>   ... yes ...
>   ... city with a hangover.[306]

The reference to a hangover, inferring that a good time was had previously, is particularly astute, referring to Liverpool's past successful commercial and maritime history when, at the time of writing, the city was clearly in a state of decline.

Liverpool makes a further appearance in *Penny Arcade* in the form of another blues poem, 'New York City Blues', dedicated to John Lennon. Lennon had been murdered in New York on 8 December 1980. Of course Henri was in the orbit of The Beatles in Liverpool in the 1960s and Roger McGough had been a member of The Scaffold with Mike McGear (McCartney), the brother of Paul McCartney. Henri was familiar with Lennon, as he attended the College of Art and was a part of that crowd alongside Stuart Sutcliffe who drank in student hangouts such as the Ye Cracke pub in Rice Street.

The murder of John Lennon had a profound effect on the city. On the Sunday following his death, a candlelit vigil was held in Liverpool. Estimates put the crowd at between 30,000 and 100,000 people, who gathered outside St George's Hall. In New York, where Lennon had lived for the final nine years of his life, an estimated 50,000 people gathered in Central Park opposite the Dakota Building where he had been murdered.

Adrian Henri had this to say about hearing the news:

> [I was] woken at seven in the morning by a friend ringing to tell me the news, fell asleep again, and really thought I'd dreamt it. When I woke up later I put the radio on and they were playing 'Beautiful Boy' and one of the lines stuck in my head about 'crossing the street [and being busy] making other plans' which struck me as being particularly ironic on that particular day.[307]

This gives us an insight into Henri's practice in writing his poem for Lennon. He clearly rated the lyrics of the song, which was written for Lennon's only child with Yoko Ono, Sean. Henri used the image of the street/road in the opening lines of his poem. Phil Bowen calls 'New York City Blues' one of the best of Henri's career. It is certainly a highlight of a long writing life.

The poem opens with three italicised lines: '*You do not cross the road/To step into immortality/An empty street is only the beginning*'[308] Over the course of its five stanzas the poem traverses a route from New York to the city of Lennon's birth forty years earlier. There is a direct reference to Lennon's famous lyric: 'Life is what happens to you/When you're busy making other plans.'[309]

This is followed by a return to the image of the empty street and the opening italicised stanza's 'only the beginning.' There is a poignancy about this poem that certainly highlights Henri's depth of feeling towards Lennon. Liverpool again makes an appearance, with reference to the riots of 1981 (indicating that the poem took a while to complete): 'Here, in your other city,/Riot vans prowl the December dark,/Remember angry embers of summer.' This stanza further emphasizes the nostalgic poignancy of the poem with its 'familiar ghost guitars echo from stucco terraces.' This is clearly a reference to the flat that Lennon shared, in Gambia Terrace, while he was an art student, with Stuart Sutcliffe (who was later to become a member of the fledgling Beatles, before leaving to focus on his art). The motif of cold pavements, roads and streets remain prevalent throughout the poem. In the 1986 *Collected Poems* version of the poem, there is a large break before the italicised final stanza. This may be due to the space constraints of the individual volume of *Penny Arcade*, but the *Collected Poems* version does feel as though it is employing a considered poetic device.

This locates us back to the scene of the murder of Lennon with '*At the dark end of the street/Waits the inevitable stranger.*'[310] Was Lennon's murder inevitable? Lennon certainly was approachable; his murderer met him earlier on the day that he shot him, to get an autograph.

The final poem in *Penny Arcade* and also in the 1986 *Collected* is 'Cat'. This long poem covers 7 pages, and, in the *Collected*, contains illustrations by Henri. The poem, perhaps amongst the most autobiographical of Henri's 1980s poems, is worth considering due to its historical contexts and references to Henri's art and relationships.

The main motif throughout the poem is the mournful mewing of a nameless cat. Henri gives us some background to the cat's origins: 'Left behind/by Fred who went to Canada, and/didn't come back.'[311] Again, the repeated motif, similar to the street motif in 'New York City Blues', focuses the reader on the importance of the cat in Henri's life, writing and art. The mix of nostalgia and references to the cat's appearance in his work is noticeable: 'Small and black./Fifteen years,/eight poems, three or four paintings.'[312] The most obvious reference in the poem is to the painting 'The Entry of Christ Into Liverpool'; the cat does not appear in the companion poem, but is there 'there, getting under the feet of heroes, friends/some now almost forgotten. You stare/out of the picture.'[313] Among those heroes and friends who appear in the painting alongside the image of the cat, are William S. Burroughs,

Charles Mingus (from whom Henri borrowed the title 'Tonight at Noon' for his 1968 debut collection), Alfred Jarry's Père Ubu, The Beatles and fellow poets, Brian Patten and Roger McGough. Another person who appears in 'Cat' and the painting 'The Entry of Christ Into Liverpool' is Heather Holden. Holden, a former student at Liverpool College of Art, met Henri while he was teaching at the college. They started a relationship, (Henri's wife Joyce was aware of the situation, and became friends with Holden) and Holden was writing poetry and reading her work around the city. 'Cat' contains some lines from a Holden poem:

'Black cat
called my
darling on
a spring day'
H.H., 2.2.1964[314]

Henri confirms the practice that the lovers had of writing poems for, and about, each other: 'Rainbow words/written from Rossendale, tucked in bright blue/envelopes.'[315] Some 'small poems [were] as warm as eggs.'[316] A draft of a Holden poem, called 'Egg Poem' was sent to Patten as a submission to his small magazine *Underdog*.[317] Perhaps, Henri was referring to this poem in his own poem nearly 20 years on. Familiar Henri subjects, travel, place(s), love, longing, sex and desire all appear in 'Cat' and this multi-dimensional poem is a prime example of Henri's poetics. Clearly autobiographical in its execution, what is interesting is the passage of time. The poem includes places such as Hope Street in Liverpool (the place of the cat's death as well as Henri's residences in Canning Street and Mount Street); Manchester; Shropshire; Paris; London; and Normandy.

Liverpool of the 1960s feeds into Liverpool of the 1980s with the fall-out from the riots present toward the end of the poem: 'Dull bell of awakening, distant smell/of burning.'[318] Clearly a poem of memory and mourning for 'Cat', the wider implications of the anonymous mewing allow Henri to reflect on his writing (and art) up to that point in his career.

The mid to late 1980s were a busy time for Henri and indeed McGough and Patten. Henri published his *Collected Poems* and collections of poetry for children (See chapter 6 for more on this aspect of his writing) and the trio of poets toured for the twentieth anniversary of *The Mersey Sound* in 1987. Henri continued touring in his own right, becoming writer in residence in Runcorn schools, Shropshire schools and at the University of Liverpool. Exhibitions of his art took place in Dublin, Bristol, London and Liverpool. He was active, as ever, in art in Liverpool. A major event, 'Pop Mechanica: Perestroika in the Avant Garde' took place in the city's Bluecoat Arts Centre in 1982. Henri's handwritten notes allude to a return to the happenings of the 1960s, with vivid references to the events that Henri co-ordinated in the city's Hope Hall.[319]

The 1980s, however, were a turbulent time for many in the arts. The Conservative government had marginalised many artists and writers through a series of cuts to the arts. Despite this, Henri became an advisor to the newly opened Tate Gallery in a former warehouse in Liverpool's Albert Dock. He would remain an advisor to the Tate until 1992. Such was Henri's draw in the 1980s, he was invited to read his poetry overseas in places such as Germany and Spain. In 1986 he met Catherine Marcangeli at a retrospective of his painting at South Hill Park Arts Centre, in Bracknell, Berkshire. Marcangeli was a French student who was travelling before heading to university. She was to play a pivotal role in Henri's life and career.

Notes

[233]For more on the John Moores Prize see http://www.liverpoolmuseums.org.uk/walker/johnmoores/

[234]Adrian Henri, *Environments and Happenings* (London: Thames and Hudson, 1974).

[235]Ibid, p117.

[236]See the appendix for the running orders of the various editions.

[237]Phil Bowen, *A Gallery to Play To*, pp. 121-2.

[238]The poem appears in *Collected Poems*, pp194-198.

[239]'Mrs Albion, You've Got a Lovely Daughter' in *Collected Poems*, pp53-54.

[240]For more about Arvon, visit its website: www.arvon.org.uk

[241]Adrian Henri in Phil Bowen, *A Gallery to Play To*, p110.

[242]Adrian Henri, 'Morning Song' from *City Hedges* in *Collected Poems*, p170.

[243]'Metropolis' from *City Hedges* in *Collected Poems*, p177.

[244]Ibid.

[245]'Metropolis' from *City Hedges* in *Collected Poems*, p179.

[246]'Poem for A.E. Housman' from *City Hedges* in *Collected Poems*, p202.

[247]A.E. Housman, *A Shropshire Lad and Other Poems* (London, Penguin Classics, 2010).

[248]'Three Landscapes' from *City Hedges* in *Collected Poems*, p203.

[249]'Butterfly' from *City Hedges* in *Collected Poems*, p206.

[250]The University of Liverpool, The Papers of Adrian Henri, Henri/8/2/9

[251]Morrissey, 'Everyday is like Sunday' from *Viva Hate* (London: His Master's Voice Records; CSD 3787), 1988.

[252]'Death in the Suburbs' from *From the Loveless Motel* in *Collected Poems*, p211.

[253]Ibid.

[254]'Death in the Suburbs' from *From the Loveless Motel* in *Collected Poems*, p212.

[255]Ibid, p213.

[256]Ibid.

[257]'From the Loveless Motel' from *From the Loveless Motel* in *Collected Poems*, pp221-228.

[258]Ibid, p223.

[259]For more about the Camel advertisement see https://www.reddit.com/r/HistoryPorn/comments/2fzzpo/new_york_new_york_the_spectacular_camel_billboard/ [accessed 29/06/16

[260]'From the Loveless Motel' from *From the Loveless Motel* in *Collected Poems*, p227.

[261]'Wasteland' from *From the Loveless Motel* in *Collected Poems*, p235. 'Wasteland' also appears in Adrian Henri, *From the Loveless Motel Poems 1976-1979*, pp36-39 and in Adrian Henri, *Selected and Published Poems 1965-2000,* ed, Catherine Marcangeli, (Liverpool: Liverpool University Press, 2007), pp128-131.

[262]T.S. Eliot, 'The Waste Land' in *The Waste Land and Other Poems* (London: Faber and Faber, 1975), p27.

[263]Adrian Henri, 'The Entry of Christ into Liverpool' in *Collected Poems*, p70.

[264]Ibid.

[265]Ibid, p69.

[266]'Notes for an Autumn Painting' from *From the Loveless Motel* in *Collected Poems*, pp220-221.

[267]'Notes for an Autumn Painting' from *From the Loveless Motel* in *Collected Poems*, p220.

[268]Ibid, p121.

[269]Phil Bowen, *A Gallery to Play To*, p131.

[270]'Autumn Leaving' from *From the Loveless Motel* in *Collected Poems*, p220.

[271]Ibid, p. 216.

[272]Ibid, p218.

[273]See Robert Hampson, *Seaport* (Exeter: Shearsman Books, 2008), p63.

[274]https://www.theguardian.com/uk/2011/dec/30/thatcher-government-liverpool-riots-1981<accessed 30/6/16>

[275]Andrew Lees, Professor of Neurology at University College, London, confirms that Henri read at the event, in an email to the author dated 5 August 2016. There are photographs of the signing at Atticus bookshop on Flickr. See < https://www.flickr.com/photos/jillmc1/albums/72157616415977351>

[276]Email from Geoff Ward to the author dated 16 August 2016.

[277]Ibid.

[278]Phil Bowen, *A Gallery to Play To*, p136.

[279]Adrian Henri, Roger McGough and Brian Patten, *New Volume* (Middlesex: Penguin Books, 1983).

[280]Letter from Robin Robertson at Penguin Books to Henri, dated 22 July 1982. The University of Liverpool, The Papers of Adrian Henri, Henri/8/2/14

[281]Letter from Adrian Henri to Roger McGough, dated 20 May 1982. The University of Liverpool, The Papers of Adrian Henri, Henri/8/2/14

[282]The University of Liverpool, The Papers of Adrian Henri, Henri/8/2/14

[283]'I Have Woken this Year' from *Penny Arcade* in *Collected Poems*, p259.

[284]Ibid.

[285]Ibid.

[286]Ibid, pp259-260.

[287]'As if in a Dream' in *Penny Arcade* in *Collected Poems*, p260.

[288]Ibid.

[289]'As if in a Dream' in *Penny Arcade* in *Collected Poems*, p261.

[290]'As if in a Dream' from *Penny Arcade* in *Collected Poems*, p261.

[291]Email from Catherine Marcangeli to the author, 18 November 2017.

[292]'As if in a Dream' from *Penny Arcade* in *Collected Poems*, p261.

[293]Ibid.

[294]'Harbour' from *Penny Arcade* in *Collected Poems*, p265.

[295]'Harbour' from *Penny Arcade* in *Collected Poems*, p271.

[296]Maurice Cockrill in Phil Bowen, *A Gallery to Play To*, p49.

[297]Jack Kerouac, *Book of Sketches, 1952-57* (New York: Penguin Books, 2006).

[298]'Rainbow' from *Penny Arcade* in *Collected Poems*, p276.

[299]'Rainbow' in *Penny Arcade* in *Collected Poems*, p276.

[300]Ibid, p277.

[301]Ibid.

[302]'Car Crash Blues *or* Old Adrian Henri's Interminable Talking Surrealistic Blues' from *Tonight at Noon and Other Poems* in *Collected Poems*, pp43-45.

[303]Ibid, pp15-16.

[304]Adrian Henri's Talking Toxteth Blues' from *Penny Arcade* in *Collected Poems*, p284.

[305]Ibid.

[306]Ibid.

[307]Adrian Henri in Phil Bowen, *A Gallery to Play To*, p130.

[308]'New York City Blues' from *Penny Arcade* in *Collected Poems*, p304.

[309]Ibid. There are several attributions to these lines. See http://quoteinvestigator.com/2012/05/06/other-plans/ for further details.

[310]'New York City Blues' from *Penny Arcade* in *Collected Poems*, p304.

[311]'Cat' from *Penny Arcade* in *Collected Poems*, p305.

[312]Ibid.

[313]Ibid.

[314]'Cat' from *Penny Arcade* in *Collected Poems*, p306.

[315]Ibid.

[316]Ibid.

[317]The University of Liverpool, The Papers of Brian Patten, Patten 1/1/3

[318]'Cat' from *Penny Arcade* in *Collected Poems*, p310.

[319]The University of Liverpool, The Papers of Adrian Henri, Henri M/2/3/1

4

A CHANGE OF DIRECTION

Wish You Were Here (1990)
and *Not Fade Away* (1994)

AFTER MEETING CATHERINE MARCANGELI, WHO WOULD become Henri's partner for the rest of his life, there was a shift in many ways. Henri became a regular visitor to France in order to spend time with Marcangeli. Henri followed her to wherever she was living: Strasbourg, Paris, Oxford and New York.

The late 1980s saw death return to Henri's door. His former wife, Joyce, died in 1987. Despite the couple having separated in the 1960s and divorcing sometime after that, they remained close and her death clearly affected Henri. The level of affection Henri still had for Joyce is evident in his next collection, *Wish You Were Here*, published by Jonathan Cape in 1990. The title had first been considered in 1982, when Henri wrote a three-page treatment for a prospective TV show titled *Wish You Were Here: A TV Programme for People and Places in Britain*. The show wasn't commissioned.[320]

Wish You Were Here was to be the end of Henri's association with Cape, which had begun with the publication of *Autobiography* in 1971. Cape got behind the publication of *Wish You Were Here* as an extensive series of readings were arranged in association with the publisher. Beginning in April 1990 with a hometown reading at Liverpool's Unity Theatre on the 11th, Henri would take to the road throughout the rest of April, and in May taking in gigs in places such as Beeston in Nottingham on the 5 May, Newbury on the 10th with Andy Roberts and Brian Patten, Winchester on the 15th, Bracknell on the 17th, Portsmouth on the 18th, and Walton-on-Thames on the 19th. Further shows with Patten and Roberts took place in Macclesfield and Manchester in June and a London date, at the Royal Festival Hall, occured in August. A further promotional push happened when BBC radio recorded in July, for later broadcast, a special *Time for Verse* show featuring Henri, who recorded twenty-one poems, including a selection from the new book as well as old favourites such as 'Love Is', 'I Want to Paint' and 'The New Fast Automatic Daffodils'.[321]

Wish You Were Here is an elegantly designed book. The cover features a collage of Henri's, including, in a facsimile of his writing, a postcard addressed to Joyce Henri. His new love, Marcangeli, appears in the top right-hand corner in the form of her passport photograph. Tickets and ephemera from places such as Hollywood, New York and Paris make the cover a visual representation of its contents. *Wish You Were Here* is dedicated 'For Joyce Henri/née Wilson/1935-1987' and contains a poem for Joyce at either end of the collection.

Opening the collection is 'For Joyce Henri, New Year 1988'. The poem begins with a series of facts regarding the ages of friends of the former couple:

> In 1987
> Willy was 40, Roger was 50, I was 55 and you
> were 52. We drank fizzy wine at your bedside
> knowing you wouldn't see 53.[322]

The poem then swiftly moves on, in the longest stanza of the three (49 lines), to the wider world away from the domestic scenario: 'In 1987/sailors died/killed by missiles fired by people not their enemies/sold them by their fellow countrymen.'[323] Death appears and is a repeated motif throughout the poem, though there is always a place for quotidian domestic nature despite impending death, with 'On July afternoons/we watched Australian soaps, quiz programmes,/you propped up in your nightdress.'[324] As one has come to expect in Henri's work, Liverpool makes an appearance: the 'ferry' and 'Cathedral square'. Catherine Marcangeli appears in the poem, 'laughed with me in Liverpool, Edinburgh, Strasbourg,/ Paris, and cried for you in London, though/she didn't know you.'[325] Travel, places such as Giverny, Belfast, Dieppe, and the USA appear, clearly shared with Marcangeli. Henri, reflecting, shares the circumstances of Joyce's death with his new love with 'strands of dark hair/in every kiss.'[326]

'Liverpool Poems' (not to be confused with the earlier poem of the same name from Henri's debut 1968 collection, *Tonight at Noon*) is a series of 6 short poems, with references to the Liverpool 8 area. In the first poem, the interaction of nature and the urban, a common theme of Henri's is evident:

> White
> under the orange lights
> a rabbit
> lopes along Hope St
> at 3 a.m.[327]

Similarly, the fourth poem mixes nature with the urban and deals with death in the city, in the form of a pigeon's death.

> a plump young pigeon
> dying in Rodney St

whistles as ineffectually
as the tramp with the penny whistle on the corner.[328]

Perhaps most pertinent is the sixth poem as it foregrounds Henri's interest in the autumn. In the opening poem of the collection, he notes 'my usual Autumn note in my notebook/about willowherb.'[329] In the sixth poem of 'Liverpool Poems', Henri locates us firmly in his Liverpool:

the last throes of summer
reflected blinding from the river
at the foot of the hill
the first hint of October
stirs poems along the cobbled street.[330]

The metaphor of poems along the street is reminiscent of 'The Entry of Christ Into Liverpool', with the 'empty chip-papers drifting round my feet.'[331] Mount Street where Henri lived was off Hope Street, which sits higher above the city, with the river below.

In typical Henri style there are plenty of love poems. This was due, in part, to a new and to be enduring love. Perhaps most intriguing are the 'Alice' poems, 'Alice/Early Autumn' and 'Alice in Winter.' The sonic qualities that Henri developed throughout his career are in evidence in the first 'Alice' poem, which describes the 'shingle-sound' of the leaves on Hope Street, which contrasts with the metallic 'tinkle' of a 'Coke-can.'[332]Again, this is reminiscent of the early Henri motifs of streets/streetscapes and of nature integrated in the urban.

In the short 'Alice/Early Autumn' there is a shift from Liverpool to London. This by itself is not unusual in Henri's canon, and we know he was a prodigious traveller, but within a short poem, it is noticeable. Perhaps we need to give consideration to who Alice (or the character of Alice), may be. Catherine Marcangeli remembers that between a relationship with Lis Burgoyne and herself, Henri had a short relationship with a woman named Alice.[333] The collection contains poems about Joyce, Lis Burgoyne and Catherine Marcangeli. While the poems for Joyce Henri and Lis Burgoyne are obvious, in the form of titles and dedications, the poems for Catherine Marcangeli are less obvious.

The second stanza of 'Alice/Early Autumn' deals with the shift to London, with its 'leafstrewn squares' and a cat 'among cat-coloured leaves'. The third stanza, half the length of the previous two, at only three lines, brings the 'you' (presumably Alice) into the poem, with her 'smile [...] like a mayfly in October.'[334] The looming death of Mayflies during the season, is perhaps Henri highlighting his concerns that this new love's days are numbered.

'Alice in Winter' is located back in Liverpool. Using the Chinese New Year as its dating point (the Chinese New Year ran from 29 January 1987 until 16 February 1988), it is easy to date the event of the poem from its first line: 'It's New Year's Day, and the Year of the Rabbit'[335] Liverpool has a large Chinese community, as noted in the introduction to this book. The city's Chinatown, the first in Europe, sits at the bottom of Upper Duke Street where it meets Nelson Street, and in the poem 'Down the hill, the Dragon capers, leaps [...]' from the perspective of Henri's home in Mount Street.[336] The city, and in particular Chinatown, is busy during the celebrations and the narrator of the poem chooses to spend the celebration indoors, making appropriate references to the year of the Rabbit: '[I] burrow[ed] into you in the darkness,/close brown warren of the bedclothes.'[337] The lovers only leave for Chinatown once the crowds have dissipated, leaving only 'torn lettuce-leaves, red messages underfoot.'[338]

This strong example of the domestic situation and sense of place is typical of *Wish You Were Here*. At the heart of the book is the sequence 'Holiday Snaps', dedicated to 'Lis'. Lis Burgoyne met Henri whilst she was writing a dissertation on his work. She was based on the Wirral peninsula eventually moving into her own place near to Henri's Mount Street home, in Little St Bride Street. Their relationship was a close one, which ended in 1986 when her thesis on Henri was completed. The 'Holiday Snaps' sequence is a series of short sketch-like poems similar to 'Rainbow', the series of poems for Maurice Cockrill, published in *Penny Arcade*. The sequence, accompanied by a sketch by Henri, is a series of short, numbered poems written during a trip Henri and Burgoyne took to America in the winter of 1985 into 1986.

The poem is written as a series of memories, begins in Liverpool and meanders its way through the landmarks of the trip, ending with memories of '*Your white toothbrush still on the shelf,/Its white travelling-case no longer travelling*'.[339] There is a subtitle to the sequence which hints at the finality of the relationship: 'black marigolds/in the desert of a long-lost summer'.[340]

The opening of the poem is located in Liverpool, and contains home life signifiers, later reiterated in the final numbered stanza; with the 'whirring of a milk float', 'bedside table' and 'the cassette alarm'.[341] It is worth noting that this forms a prequel to the numbered stanzas that follow, highlighting its importance to grounding the reader in the scenario of the poem. The first numbered stanza locates the reader in Sunset Heights, California, with its 'cactus' and 'cypresses/piled stark up/against implacable blue'.[342] This naturalistic, painterly introduction to the sequence sets the tone for what is to follow. This overtly naturalistic sketch (which may or may not be the accompanying sketch in the book), gives way to the gritty urban hyper-surreal and unreal nature of Los Angeles. A trip to Universal Studios (a ticket appears on the cover collage) brings the reader's attention to the vagaries of

America, with the 'GlamTram' and 'the giant shark attacks;/later I pose by his concrete carcase [...]'[343]

The third stanza is of interest, as it is another example of Henri switching the narrative focus of the poem to Liverpool. Rather like 'Alice in Winter' or the opening part to 'Holiday Snaps', we are firmly positioned in Santa Monica with 'SEE CONAN THE DESTROYER written on the sky.' While the advertising shifts to Liverpool:

> Today the airship saying FUJIFILM
> that spied you there in your grey striped bikini
> drifts aimlessly across the Mersey.[344]

There is a tonal and geographical shift from '6' to '12', to New York and the pace of the poems slows with a certain sense of melancholy. The place names such as Bleeker [sic] Street, Leroy Street, the East Village and Washington Square, alongside narrator-led descriptions such as 'Graffiti city', and 'tiny picnic-lights blossom,/effortless as skyscrapers', [...]' and 'Tears like New York summer rain' contribute to a sense of familiarity which doesn't detract from the sentimental aspects of the individual poems.[345]

The final stanza describes the preparations for leaving. There is the familiar Henri reference to music:

> 'I want to know what love is'
> implores the muzak in the morning bank
> 'I want you to show me'[346]

The final stanza switches from the New York location, through Cheshire with its 'bright eyed speedwell' and 'forget – you – not' to Liverpool and then Normandy.[347] The stanza is broken by a single word line, 'remember', which gives way to the italicised domestic scenario noted above. There is a reiteration of the senses over the two final stanzas that neatly brings the poem to a satisfying climax:

Tears like neon city rain

Lost sunset heights
of summer.[348]

Liverpool makes a prominent return to the book in the 'Morning, Liverpool 8', which Phil Bowen considers atypical of Henri's Liverpool poems, as it 'anthropomorphizes his neighbourhoods' terraces'. But the poem is much more than that, and despite Bowen's reading, it fits neatly into the Henri canon of Liverpool poems.[349] We can trace these poems back to *The Mersey Sound* and Henri's debut collection, *Tonight at Noon.* Perhaps the closest counterpoint to 'Morning, Liverpool 8' is 'Liverpool 8' with its similar descriptions of the wonderful Georgian architecture that fills the area. In 'Morning, Liverpool 8', Henri allows the buildings a persona: they come alive as if after a slumber. This gives a clue as to the poem's central message, a glance over the shoulder to the riots and the former glories of the area's past with 'distant dreams of hopscotch,/ hoofbeats on cobblestones'. The 'nightmare of bulldozers,/dripping water, charred beams' tells of the 1981 events. Revealingly, Henri has two streets within Liverpool 1 'tell' of the recent events: 'Hope Place/and Huskisson tell of the nightmare almost gone'.[350] Interestingly, Henri chooses to not give Huskisson Street its full name. This is to personify the name, after the street was named after William Huskisson, a former MP of Liverpool and now mainly remembered for being the world's first railway casualty.[351]

The title poem of the collection is an eight-part sequence typical of this later period of Henri's work. A travelogue poem, the places mentioned at the foot of each poem are Izmir (Turkey); Cappadocia (Turkey); Fuentevaqueros (Spain); Granada (Spain); Sitges (Spain); Barcelona (Spain) and Troy (Greece). Tellingly, number 7 is without a location. It is obviously for Joyce Henri:

> *One of the two*
> *I always sent*
> *was to you:*
> *now there's only one*
> *to do.*[352]

It is reminiscent of an early poem, 'Poem for Roger McGough', which featured in *The Mersey Sound*, *Tonight at Noon* and *Selected and Unpublished*:

> A nun in a Supermarket
> Standing in the queue
> Wondering what it's like
> To buy groceries for two.[353]

This plays on McGough's seven-lined poem 'Vinegar' which closes with the lines 'quietly thinking/as the vinegar runs through/ how nice it would be/to buy supper for two'.[354]

The tone of *Wish You Were Here* is reflective and, overall, rather melancholic. There is, however, a slight and welcome interlude. Number '4' titled *A Scouser in Spain for James Fenton*:

> 'Hey, lad,
> is there a Heladeria
> round here?'[355]

The colloquialism of 'lad' and abbreviation of 'round' combined with the absurdist notion of asking for an ice-cream parlour in Spain in that language, works well in breaking the reportage and slightly melancholic feeling of the sequence as a whole.

In 'Visiting Writer', Henri revisits his favourite season – autumn in a wistful poem that reminisces about visiting Catherine Marcangeli, possibly, in her student rooms. The bold opening lines gives us the mental state of the narrator:

Sunday, and seven weeks
without a drink. I think of you
in another town. Outside the leaves
turn brown. [...]356

The internal rhyme does little to distract here. Again, matching the melancholic elements of the autumn season, Henri highlights this feeling of isolation with 'I see your little student room/almost identical to this one. Summer gone,/and not a hangover to show for it', while 'across the campus poems fall in September sunlight/ like sober bells'.357 The dual meaning of 'sober' works to highlight the fact that the narrator has not been drinking, while the sober nature of bells ringing links well with the seasonal elements, and shortening days. The enjambment in 'Visiting Writer' is interesting as it draws on the influence of William Carlos Williams, whose short lines, usually without punctuation, would allow for the reader to grasp the Williamsian idea that a poem 'is a small (or large) machine made out of words'. What is perhaps more interesting when it comes to thinking about Henri and, in particular, 'Visiting Writer', is what else Williams says. He argues that 'there is nothing sentimental about a machine [...] When I say there's nothing sentimental about a poem, I mean that there can be no part that is redundant.'358 There is nothing wasteful in 'Visiting Writer' – everything has a purpose.

Following 'Visiting Writer' is another of Henri's 'Painting' poems. In a similar vein to 'Rainbow', the poem for Maurice Cockrill, 'Four Studies of Dieppe' is dedicated to 'the painter Nicholas Horsfield'. Horsfield, a contemporary of Henri's, was described by the *Independent* as a 'leading Liverpool painter', was part of the Liverpool College of Art scene, and taught Stuart Sutcliffe and John Lennon.359 The *Guardian*, meanwhile, called Horsfield a 'painter's painter' and 'one of the most influential members of the Merseyside art world'.[360] The title of Henri's poem is appropriate. Horsfield was a regular visitor to the French port Dieppe, which he first visited in 1956, and he continued to make trips there, throughout his life.[361]

As the title suggests, 'Four Studies of Dieppe' is painterly in its execution. Arranged neatly on the page, the four parts, each numbered, are four lines long. Familiar observations about landscape, nature and, of course, colour, permeate the poems. The fourth 'study' makes reference to the Battle of Normandy during World War II. The port remained occupied during the battle until the Germans left their posts on 1 September 1944 after the Canadian infantry landed. The fourth study notes the 'zinc white' and 'the green-capped stones' and implores us to 'remember the suck of boots,/the crunch of landingcraft'.[362]

A further poem about loss appears in the form of 'The Bell'. A timely poem, in terms of its response to an event, 'The Bell' deals with the city of Liverpool's grief after the Hillsborough Disaster. Liverpool FC (of whom Henri was a supporter) played an FA Cup semi-final tie against Nottingham Forest FC at Sheffield Wednesday's Hillsborough stadium, on 15 April 1989. Due to police negligence, as the final inquest between 2014 and 2016 found, 96 Liverpool supporters died through overcrowding and crushing inside the stadium. The city's response to the disaster was one of uniting in grief. Everton FC, Liverpool FC's neighbours in the city, led a walk between the two grounds of Goodison Park and Anfield, where supporters gathered to lay flowers in front of the Liverpool home supporters' stand, The Kop.

Henri's poem, written as a response to hearing the Cathedral bell from his home in nearby Mount Street, is startling in its imagery. The opening line, 'The bell, tolled all afternoon/we did not send to ask/for whom' works on two levels.[363] The Cathedral bell rang once for each person who died (94 died on the day of the disaster, and 2 died later due to their injuries) and therefore would have been noticeably different to the usual calling for prayer. 'We did not send to ask/for whom' works as a throwback to the traditional sign from a local church that somebody has died, alongside another echo of the past in the form of a line from John Donne's 'For Whom the Bell Tolls', but in this case, the community at large has been affected and this is represented by 'it tolls for you'.[364] The bell [told] 'of flowers/heaped in a goalmouth [...] it told of/eyes like TV screens/haunted by last night's images [...]'[365] The central image of the bell tolling is both sombre and fitting and carries on in the narrator's thoughts well into evening:

> the deep bell
> still tolled in our heads
> long after the light had gone.[366]

Wish You Were Here ends with another poignant poem about Joyce Henri. Simply titled 'For Joyce' this is an elegiac 7-lined, single stanza work, complete with Joyce's words. The opening line is effective in its unobtrusiveness:

> 'I don't want
> to be any trouble' you'd say,
> every day.[367]

The repetition which follows, vociferous in its execution, is almost disbelieving: 'Don't want to be any trouble' could be read as the recipient's question. It is more likely to be the speaker's protestation, and is beautifully answered by:

> [...] If you don't want
> to be any trouble,
> why do you walk into my dreams
> every night?[368]

'For Joyce' is a fitting end to a strong collection of work. The death of Joyce Henri and the Hillsborough Disaster had a profound effect on Henri. He had previously painted the Kop at Anfield in 1977, in a painting named 'Kop II'. A companion painting, 'Flowers for Liverpool', followed, days after the disaster in 1989, and is a poignant painting of the floral tributes that were placed in the football stadium in the days of the disaster. The painting is now housed in Liverpool FC's museum.[369]

The early 1990s saw Henri receive an honorary D.Litt from Liverpool Polytechnic (now Liverpool John Moores University). He undertook readings in Spain and the Netherlands and travelled to such places as Jordan and the USA. Of course, poetry and paintings would emerge from these travels. In 1992 he visited Senegal and was a participant at the Gorée International Poetry Festival. An interesting aside is that Gorée had been an important slave trading centre, and a series of large warehouses named after Gorée had been built near the waterfront in Liverpool – built in 1793 and eventually demolished in the 1950s.

Henri also continued to show his art in solo and group shows around the UK including in Liverpool, London and Lancaster. At the show at the Orrell Arts Centre in Bootle, north Liverpool, Henri showed a series of the nature paintings that he had recently been working on. One particular painting sticks in the mind. Bootle Library, across the town and located on one of the main roads to Liverpool city centre, had in its window a large Henri work, 'Rapefield'. This mesmeric work stood out greatly in the urban environment of a busy main road. Henri had this to say about the painting:

> This painting is very much to do with the part of my life which is spent travelling on trains. Over the last ten years or so we've seen the European rape seed phenomenon.

What others see as a curse I found a blessing visually – this shock of yellow coming through a carriage window.[370]

In 1993 Catherine Marcangeli moved to New York. This meant frequent trips to the city for Henri and resulted in a series of paintings. Always a notebook poet, by his own admission, these trips also gave Henri the opportunity to work on new poetry.

Henri's next collection, *Not Fade Away*, was published by Bloodaxe Books, considered by many to be one of the top five UK poetry publishers. The company's website declares itself 'Britain's premier poetry imprint.'[371] It was set up in 1978 by founder Neil Astley, and has published titles by poets such as Nobel Prizewinner Tomas Tranströmer, J.H. Prynne and Tess Gallagher. Henri signed the contract with Bloodaxe for *Not Fade Away* on 28 January 1994, having previously delivered the manuscript extant.[372]

The title *Not Fade Away* builds on the previous collection's title *Wish You Were Here*, with the new book's title coming from a song. 'Not Fade Away' was written by Buddy Holly and recorded in 1957.[373] It is an apt title for what would become Henri's final collection of work to be published during his lifetime.

The cover features a detail of the painting 'The Entry of Christ into Liverpool' and the title of the book is followed by 'Poems 1989-1994'. In a cropped section of the painting, highlighted on the front cover, are the words 'Live Socialism' from the banner 'Long live Socialism' alongside Père Ubu, and James Ensor as Christ. The rear cover image is partially obscured by the blurb. This blurb, which states that *Not Fade Away* is 'about preserving memories, in various ways: of favourite artworks; of friends and heroes [...] of a continuing, international love affair.'[374] On the rear cover Carol Ann Duffy notes that:

This warm personal collection reads like a book of days. There are

> poems for Elvis, André Breton and Debussy, postcards from
> Normandy, Africa and the States; alongside lyrics for lost friends
> and times, and for new loves, which speak with a direct simplicity.[375]

The book is dedicated 'For Catherine, in whatever country we are'. Again, there are love poems and, as Carol Ann Duffy mentions in her blurb, there are more travel poems, in which the destination of travel was in part determined by Marcangeli's location. Aside from being a collection of poems dated from 1989-1994, *Not Fade Away* is ordered into four sections: 'A Portrait of the Artist', 'Souvenirs', 'Yosemite' and 'Look, Stranger ... ' This allows the poems to be strictly ordered and harks back to the layout of *Autobiography* in 1971.

Not Fade Away begins in a similar vein to *Wish You Were Here*, with a poem of loss. 'A Portrait of the Artist' is dedicated, in memoriam, to Henri's friend and fellow artist, Sam Walsh. Walsh, who died in 1989, was a major player in the Liverpool art scene of the 1960s. One of his most famous paintings, 'The Dinner Party' (which is now in the permanent collection of Liverpool's Walker Art Gallery) features Walsh with 22 others around a dinner table. Henri is one of the 22. Walsh appears in the painting of 'The Entry of Christ Into Liverpool' and is foregrounded on the cover of *Not Fade Away*. 'A Portrait of the Artist', with its overtures to James Joyce's *A Portrait of the Artist as a Young Man*, is a vivid recollection of Walsh and his work. It is loaded with references of Liverpool and filled with allusions to popular cultural and political figures such as John Wayne, Ingrid Bergman, General Norman Schwarzkopf and Saddam Hussain. Of course, the 'first' Gulf War, which ran from August 1991 to February 1992, was fresh in the mind.

'A Portrait of the Artist' begins by locating itself in 'a forgotten attic smelling faintly of soot' where a portfolio ('where the artist kept his dreams') is 'linked by cobwebs, flakes of plaster,/the mummified bodies of spiders [...]'[376] The second stanza, ghostly in its content, locates paintings around Liverpool. Walsh was known as a semi-realist painter of portraits (the National Portrait Gallery in London houses his portrait of Paul McCartney called *Mike's Brother* in its permanent collection) and describes a portrait of Ingmar Bergman with vivid, lined descriptions. Tellingly there is:

> a final dream
> the artist did not dream,
> of paintings of Saddam Hussain
> and General Norman Schwarzkopf
> huge as war memorials.[377]

The third stanza describes the portrait of the artist that provides the title of the poem. It is a vivid description and likeness of Walsh as seen on the cover of the book, 'black beard trimmed neatly,/ high cheekbones, dark hair falling/across his forehead.'[378] The poem continues to describe the portrait and the model also featured in the painting.

The final stanza returns the reader's attention to the attic, where '[the dust] stirs for a moment,/then settles; a few tiny motes/catch the late afternoon sunlight.'[379] There is a sense of longing and loss at the closing of the day, rather like the tradition of the last post being played in the Belgian town of Ypres every evening. Walsh and Henri exhibited their work together in Liverpool at the Hanover Gallery in 1986, three years before Walsh's death.

The painterly theme continues in the first section, in the poem 'Honeysuckle, Butterfly, Rose'.[380] With an epigraph from D.G. Rossetti, 'And her far seas moan as a single shell,/And her grove glow with love-lit fires of Troy', the poem is also '*after D.G. Rossetti: "Venus Verticordia"*'. The poem is a literal writing through of the painting, as Henri acknowledges.[381]

Henri's poem, whose title is taken from three component parts of the painting, is a 10-stanza poem that is punctuated by chorus-like refrain. Henri mixes these lines up each time they are employed in the poem, in an almost cut-up manner. For example, the first chorus reads: '*Honeysuckle, butterfly, rose,/apple and dart*' whilst the final interlude (and final stanza) reads: '*Honeysuckle, butterfly,/ butterfly, rose*'.[382] These selected natural items, are all prominent in the painting. Rossetti's sonnet that accompanies the poem, first appeared in an essay by Algernon Swinburne titled 'Notes on the Royal Academy Exhibition'[383] and is used by Henri as the starting point for his own poem. Though not a sonnet, Henri's poem follows a form (a three-line stanza followed by a two-line cut-up, a repeated refrain) and follows the meaning of the original title (translated from the Latin, to mean 'Venus, Turner of Hearts' or 'who burns hearts'). While Rossetti took this literally the opposite way, showing a femme fatale, Henri grounds his reader in the images of desire.[384]

The opening stanza describes Venus as she appears in Rossetti's painting:

> Golden aureole, palest areola
> more delicate than roses,
> hair haloed with brimstone butterflies[385]

Here there is a dual effect, the halo equating with holiness, while the aureole is sensuous.

It is known that this painting is the only example of a Rossetti nude, and also that he had great difficulty painting roses. It seems fitting that Henri focuses on the form of Venus comparing her to the roses that Rossetti laboured over.

The poem continues in a similar manner in the second stanza:

> Heart cleansed of all

but the sight of white breasts
prouder than envious flowers[386]

Whose heart has been 'cleansed' is a little ambiguous. Rossetti only reveals one breast in the painting; the other is covered by Venus's hand which is holding the dart and apple. The third stanza takes its cue from Rossetti's sonnet, allowing for the image of flora to inhabit the lines Henri quoted in the preface: 'Coarse stamens strain/for that dark grove where far seas moan, as in a single shell.' The strong sibilance of the opening line gives rise to the Rossetti lines and keeps the reader in touch with the central image of Rossetti's painting and sonnet.

Further poems in the opening section of *Not Fade Away* are dedicated to artists and popular cultural figures, such as André Breton, Claude Debussy and Elvis Presley. In a similar vein to Henri's 'Blues' poems, 'Blue for Slim' (in memoriam Slim Galliard), the poem highlights one of Galliard's most famous songs 'Cement Mixer (Put-Ti Put-Ti)'. A highly rhythmic poem, that apes the song's structure, 'Blue for Slim', and the double meaning of its title (blue as in mournful for the passing of the musician, alongside the blues as a musical genre), the poem refers to Greek mythology with 'Lethe's shore', Lethe being one of the rivers of the underworld, Hades and also the personification of forgetfulness and oblivion, in the shape of a goddess. This is the opening stanza:

Cement mixer don't putty-putty no more
Cement mixer don't putty-putty no more
Cos my man Slim has gone to Lethe's shore[387]

The repetition and indeed layout of the poem, with its strict rhyme, echoes the blues form. Combined with the repetition of the first stanza as the final stanza albeit italicised, the poem further emulates the song-like blues, with the form becoming a tribute to the musician. Henri takes the opportunity to shift the poem from New York (52nd Street; the jazz area of the city from 1920 through to the 1950s) to Liverpool and 'Dunkin' bagels back in Liverpool town/Thinking of Slim as the Mersey sun goes down'. The image of the sun going down, combined with the rhyme of town and down, works particularly well at the poem's finale, in repeating the blues rhythmic and rhyming structure.

The title poem of section two, 'Souvenirs', is dedicated to John and Anne Willett. John Willett was a friend of Henri's as far back as when the Happenings were staged in Liverpool in the early 1960s and was to remain a friend of Henri's until the poet's death in 2000; Willett died in 2002. Willett's book *Art in a City*, which he researched during a stay in Liverpool in the 1960s, and published in 1967, was re-issued in 2007 featuring, rather fittingly, Henri's 'The Entry of Christ into Liverpool' as the cover image.[388] Willett had a varied and long journalistic career writing for the *Guardian* and he was deputy editor of the *Times Literary Supplement* for a time. He was vociferous in his support for Henri and had this to say about his poetry:

> He's certainly not straightforward, but always fresh with an energy and a generosity, unlike so many poets, that is not only concerned with pushing his own work, but others that he respects. He has never believed in any arts hierarchy in which he's forced to fit into.[389]

The Willetts had a holiday home in Normandy and Henri was a regular house guest over the years; 'Souvenirs' is a memory poem. It is loaded, as you would expect, with visual images and the details that perhaps only painters notice: 'Chocolate sardines, torn election-posters MAR/CHAIS'[390] The splitting over lines of the name of the leader of the French Communist Party (PCF), Georges Marchais, and the capitalisation of his name, hints at the torn nature of the poster. Marchais stood as a Presidential candidate in 1981.

In a similar way, the narrator's eye sees 'the yellow-and-grey world', 'lemon light', 'night hydrangeas' and at the end of the stanza, 'Blinding/rain that wipes away the cliffs at Etretat.'[391] Further memories appear: 'A black workman's suit, a sailor's cap/bought beside St Jacques [...] Each stone that I have brought home/since 1968'. The whole sensory nature of the poem is brought to the fore with 'Late light across the harvestfields/from Ambrumesnil. Cattle dream, creamy as caramel./The smell across the valley from the Nescafé factory'.[392]

The final stanza, three lines in length compared to the first and second stanzas with their nine lines, highlights the importance of memory to Henri. Though it is hinted at earlier in the poem, the final stanza and its fixed notion of memory equated with the passage of time is worth quoting in full:

> The tall gingko tree that split ten years ago,
> one twin trunk that still lies overgrown,
> immutable as memory.[393]

The collection then takes a different turn. Shifting locations from the French coast to America and its Death Valley, Henri returns to poems, with a heavy reliance on puns, which made up so much of his early writing. Sharing a page with another poem, something that is at odds with Henri's practice in previous Cape publications, 'Death Valley' plays on Psalm 23, 'The Lord is My Shepherd'. Following the archaic beginning of the psalm: 'Yea', the shift from foot power in the form of walking, to automotive power is at first quite disarming, yet funny:

> Yea, though I drive
> airconditioned

> through the Valley of the Shadow
> of Death [...][394]

The real alteration from the Psalm is in the final lines: 'Nissan and Misubishi [sic]/do not comfort me.'[395] The suggestion here, is that despite the comfort of the air conditioning, thought is given over to the early pioneers, travelling through the brutal locale, without such luxuries – the air conditioning is evidently failing due to the heat.

Another travel poem, 'Impressions d'Afrique', came out of Henri's trip to Senegal in 1992 and the Gorée International Poetry Festival. With four titled and numbered parts, the first of which is *Chaloupe* (French for small wooden boat, not a proper boat), the poem is a presented in a simple narrative structure re-telling the trip: the arrival, the conference and departure. Loosely rhymed, and written in short lines *Chaloupe* does a good job in setting the scene of the poem with vivid description:

> images that avoid me,
> bright flamboyant
> as a Poinciana tree,
> the light
> on the still-misted sea.[396]

Part II of the poem, *Conference*, uses the purpose of the trip alongside the image of new wine being placed in old wine bottles, as its core, with the notion that what has gone before is being repeated:

> We talk of tradition
> putting new wine
> in old bottles.[397]

Fellow poets and their poetics are mentioned: 'For Hawad/the poem is the marks/left by tent-pegs/when the camp has moved on.'[398] Hawad appears to be the poet sometimes known as Mahmoudan Hawad, born in Niger.[399]

Part III, *Departure*, another loosely-rhymed seven-lined stanza, personifies the sun, which speaks in French: '*Bonjour, çava?*' 'and stays, persistent as/the vendors who won't go away [...]'[400]

The final part, *A Poem instead of a Postcard*, is reminiscent of Henri's earlier prose poem, 'Hello Adrian (for Adrian Mitchell)'[401] in that there is a definite addressee, in this case Janine. The layout is in the formal layout of a letter:

> Dear Janine,
>   A postcard from the edge
> of Africa. *Impressions d'Afrique.*[402]

The poem highlights that memories 'come and go, regular as the ferry', and the ever present Henri theme of love is never far away; [memories] 'regular as thoughts of her, despite/the catwalk grace of girls on the beach [...]'[403]

The poem then further descends into the language of the postcard with its layout:

> I sit on the terrace for hours. The fish
> is delicious. Can't wait to paint
> the flowers. I want to stay.
>   love,
>   A[404]

The intimation that the trip has been influential and productive for the painter/poet, is brought to the fore with the simple, informal line 'Can't wait to paint/the flowers' alongside the familiar travel trope of not wanting to leave.[405]

In 1991 Henri visited Jordan. The trip produced paintings and forms part of the long sequence of travel poems, split between (and dated by Henri as April-October 1991) Jordan and Liverpool, titled

'From an Antique Land'. Formed of 10 stanzas of various lengths, some titled and some not, 'From an Antique Land' sees Henri back on familiar ground. Reminiscent of the sequences previously written and dedicated to fellow artists such as Nicholas Horsfield and Maurice Cockrill, the location of each poem is signposted in italics at the end. Colour appears to the fore in most of the poems. Number 2 seems slightly more concerned with wider issues than the other poems. While it begins with the narratorial voice describing the person who is waiting 'patient at the gate/for us, tattooed patterns/on her face', the focus soon shifts to the child, 'who clings to her black skirts' and who is wearing a Mickey Mouse t-shirt.[406] This feels like a comment on globalisation, whereby the West meets a country with a middle-eastern feel, deemed as being at the crossroads of Asia, Europe and Africa, and marks its presence with its cultural signifiers.

There is also a short haiku-esque love poem footnoted '*for Catherine*' that is reminiscent of the shorter poems from the 1960s with brand names present, in this case 'Vaseline', as '[my] lips dry/for lack of your kisses'.[407]

The untitled ninth poem, located in 'Quasr Amara/Petra', juxtaposes religious imagery with landscape: 'The Caliph sits in majesty/above the dancing-girls, the graffiti' and there is the 'rising of the moon,/a sugared almond in the sky' while the tenth poem, 'Aphrodite', 'dances to unheard music/in a museum case/in Liverpool'.[408] This again alludes to the East-West dichotomy.

The third section of the book, 'Yosemite', deals with yet more memories and travel pieces, as the title may suggest. Early in the selection there is a nod to one of Henri's poetic heroes, William Carlos Williams. 'The Cerise Swimsuit (after William Carlos Williams)' uses the opening lines of one of Williams' most famous poems, 'The Red Wheelbarrow'. It is important to see the layout as presented by both Williams and Henri:

> So much depends
> upon[409]

The rest of 'The Cerise Swimsuit' follows Williams' poem stylistically, and to the initiated it would be recognisable as a tribute to Williams.[410] A painting, 'Skyline With Swimsuit, California', partly shared the title of the poem, and indeed is a painting of a cerise swimsuit. The painting was executed on a visit to Los Angeles with Marcangeli in 1992. In a draft of 'The Cerise Swimsuit' housed in The Liverpool Poets archive at the University of Liverpool, Henri has handwritten Williams' 'The Red Wheelbarrow' next to the draft of his poem.[411] In the catalogue of the retrospective exhibition held in Liverpool's Walker Art Gallery in 2000, Henri said this about the poem: 'So it's a kind of left-handed tribute to one of the greatest masters of modern poetry as well as commemorating a holiday experience.[412]

Memory appears again in the poem 'Thicket'. There is a sense of melancholy that runs through this poem, as the narrator casts his mind back to childhood and in particular, the perspective and size of woodlands. The layout, once again, appears to derive influence from William Carlos Williams, by its use of enjambment:

> Like
> the childhood undergrowth
> of woods
> shrunk now
> to an average-sized coppice [...][413]

The excitement of being in the woodland is obvious in the poem: 'the thrill/still lurks within [...].'[414] The personification of the wood, 'to the dark heart within,/warm, amniotic' leads to the final line, reminiscent of 'Portrait of the Artist': 'smell, faint and distinct/as memory.'[415] The poem feels like a study for a painting. Indeed, Henri did a series of hedgerow paintings (see chapter 3 for more on this).

'Oxford, Sunday, Rain' another composite travel, love and memory poem, catches effortlessly the leaving behind of a loved one. Though not specifically noted as being autumn, there is an autumnal feel surrounding the poem, with its 'Wet quadrangles', and 'Backpacked tourists' that 'huddle/in their anoraks'.[416] The university location of the poem, alongside the repeated line 'It is always like this', highlights the wrench of leaving, alongside the dialogue within the poem: 'I'll ring when I get back. See you soon', is evidence that this is a poem about visiting Catherine Marcangeli, who worked at the University of Oxford between 1990 and 1992. The poem, presented as a single stanza, strays from merely being a poem of recollection, with a hint of the lyric: 'Dreaming choirs of birds/sing evensong in the evening garden/between your room.'[417]

The final section of the book, titled 'Look, Stranger ... ' begins with a sequence that shares the title of the section, which in itself, comes from a famous line from W.H. Auden: 'Look, stranger, at this island now ... '[418] The six poems of the sequence are similar in nature to the sketch poems that appeared in *Wish You Were Here*. There is an underlying theme, of passing strangers, aside from 'Rhyl Sands' which is dedicated to David Cox and Martin O'Connor. The stranger of the poem, 'Indolent', as the opening line has it (it is the only word in the opening line too, thus drawing attention to its importance) is reading Nietzsche's *Thus Spake Zarathustra* with his personal stereo that 'pollutes the air like cigarette-smoke'.[419] The crux of the problem is that the young man appears to be not noticing the landscape beyond the window, with its 'blazing candlewick/of rapefields, the punctual mayblossom,/the bright lodges.'[420] We see a return to the Henri mode of compound words, stemming from his awareness of the modernist tradition, and so reminiscent of aspects of the earlier poetry. Perhaps the date of the poem is important here. 1 May, or May Day, is traditionally a spring festival day in the northern hemisphere, yet is more commonly known as International Workers' Day. Henri may have been making a comment on the 'youth of today', being easily distracted away from the beauty of the natural world.

'Two Pastorales' are very reminiscent of the earlier Henri sketches, though they are lightweight in tone, with easy and obvious rhymes – 'hat' and 'that'; 'trees' and 'breeze'. They focus on strangers – a 'foreman' and 'a peterade of tractors', typically un-Henri like images, focusing on machinery that manages nature. The 'I' appears in the final poem, '*Fin de Vacances*' (End of Holiday) and captures the realisation that 'The holidays are over' along with the 'unmeant "see-you-next-years" said' and the return to normal life with 'straw hats pushed to the back of wardrobes'.[421] Perhaps, the final two lines best capture that moment when the holiday is over and life returns to some form of normality:

> Now, something nice out of a tin, and telly,
> and start again.[422]

The return to domesticity, something that most returning travellers can relate to, is enhanced by the alliterative qualities of that tightly punctuated penultimate line.

This sense of domesticity is highlighted again in the collection, in 'Annus Mirabilis'. The title of a John Dryden poem of 1667, this Latin phrase, meaning 'wonderful year', is perhaps, most famously associated with Philip Larkin's poem of the same name.[423] Henri cleverly riffs on the opening stanza of Larkin's poem, switching the opening line: 'sexual intercourse began/in nineteen sixty-three' becomes 'Gourmet eating began/in nineteen sixty-three'.[424] Similarly, the final reiterative stanza uses Larkin's final stanza as a model. At the heart of Henri's poem, as indicated by the opening line, is food. It is loco-specific, with references to the local Liverpool dish of scouse and 'a Somali café/called *The Verlyn*, to begin with;/ soon to change to *The Silver Moon*'.[425] Liverpool has had a large Somalian community since the nineteenth century when Somalis signed up for the British Royal Navy. This demographic rose after the outbreak of the Somalian civil war in 1991 with people seeking asylum. Pointing to the pre-decimalised currency, locating the reader to 1963, we are given a breakdown of this 'gourmet' eating:

> Meat curry half-a-crown,
> the cheapest meal in town:
> and sixpence more for chicken,
> as a treat.[426]

Joyce Henri appears in the poem, cooking 'Paprika Chicken/ made by Joyce when times were good;/not much choice when they weren't.'[427]

Henri's left-wing politics returned to the fore in 1992. 'Winter's Ending' was first published in the Labour Party's election manifesto in April 1992, commissioned by the Labour Party.[428] The general election took place on 9 April 1992. According to the manifesto, Henri wrote the poem in March.[429] The mood in the UK leading up to the election was one of expectation: a change was in the air. After a Conservative led government since 1979, and the removal of Margaret Thatcher as Prime Minister by her own party in November 1990, the consensus was that a Labour Party victory was imminent, though it was not to happen.

'Winter's Ending', seventeen lines long, with its title insinuating that the dark days are over, begins with an unattributed quotation as its opening line: 'A cold coming we had of it'. The line is the opening line of T.S. Eliot's 'The Journey of the Magi'.[430] The overall tone of 'Winter's Ending' is bleak. There are obvious negatives: 'cardboard cities' is a reference to the cardboard city erected by the homeless in the Waterloo area of London that existed from the early 1980s until a cinema was built on the land in 1998. References to government cuts appear in the form of 'shared books in leaking classrooms' and 'crammed into peeling waiting-rooms'.[431] A sense of optimism manifests with the emergence in the poem of the title on a line of its own followed by a colon: 'factories open like daffodils,/trains flex frozen rheumatic joints [...] as the last of the cardboard boxes/are swept away beneath busy bridges'.[432] It is worth mentioning the nod that Henri gives to the flower that appears most in his work – the daffodil. Perhaps the strongest lines are left to the end. Here, the allusion to winter and the blue of thirteen years of Conservative rule (Blue being the colour of that party) being eclipsed by the new dawn and emergence of the Labour party, is particularly elevating: 'the cold blue landscape of winter/suddenly alive with bright red roses'. The rose was the emblem of the Labour Party at that time.[433]

As with Cape's backing of *Wish You Were Here*, Bloodaxe appears to have got behind the promotion of *Not Fade Away*. Henri was, as ever, busy before, during and after the publication of the book holding workshops and readings in places such as Macclesfield, Warrington and Birkenhead in March of 1994.

After visiting Catherine Marcangeli in New York in May, there were readings with McGough and Patten in Brentford and Liverpool in June. Immediately after the publication of *Not Fade Away* Henri visited Rotterdam for a week. Travel, as ever, was a major part of Henri's life. He finished the year with more shows with McGough and Patten in Blackheath and Blackpool, spent a week with Carol

Ann Duffy teaching an Arvon Course in Totleigh Barton in Devon, and held a week of workshops in Liverpool schools.

Though not as successful a collection as *Wish You Were Here*, *Not Fade Away* is important in the sense that it was Henri's final collection while he was alive. The book certainly has its moments, with strong poems such as 'Oxford, Sunday, Rain' and 'Winter's Ending'. However, it feels as though Henri was experimenting with the idea of sectioning the book, something he had previously successfully achieved with his pamphlet publications, yet ultimately, as a final collection, it feels somewhat slight, after the cohesiveness of *Wish You Were Here*. Thankfully, with the publication of *Selected and Unpublished* in 2007, Henri's stronger final poems would see the light of day.

Notes

[320]The University of Liverpool, The Papers of Adrian Henri, Henri 8/2/10

[321]BBC contract accessed at The Liverpool Poets archive, the University of Liverpool, 12 December 2016.

[322]'For Joyce Henri, New Year 1988' in *Wish You Were Here* (London: Cape, 1990), p1.

[323]Ibid.

[324]'For Joyce Henri, New Year 1988' in *Wish You Were Here*, p1.

[325]'For Joyce Henri, New Year 1988' in *Wish You Were Here*, p2.

[326]Ibid.

[327]Adrian Henri, 'Liverpool Poems' in *Wish You Were Here*, p6. 'Liverpool Poems' also appears in *Liverpool Accents: Seven Poets and a City*, ed. Peter Robinson, pp47-48, and in Adrian Henri, *Selected and Unpublished Poems 1965-2000*, ed. Catherine Marcangeli, pp134-135.

[328]Adrian Henri, 'Liverpool Poems' in *Wish You Were Here*, p6. This also

refers to a series of paintings and collages that Henri had made in the 1960s. The three pieces of art are 'Death of a Bird in the City, 1961', 'Death of a Bird in the City, 1964-5' and 'Night Door (Homage to Djuna Barnes), 1964-5'. For more about these artworks see Adrian Henri, *Adrian Henri: Paintings 1953-1998*, pp42-45.

[329]'For Joyce Henri, New Year 1988' in *Wish You Were Here*, p1.

[330]Adrian Henri, 'Liverpool Poems' in *Wish You Were Here*, p7.

[331]Adrian Henri, 'The Entry of Christ into Liverpool' in *Collected Poems*, p71.

[332]'Alice / Early Autumn' in *Wish You Were Here*, p11.

[333]Email from Catherine Marcangeli to the author, 18 November 2017.

[334]'Alice / Early Autumn' in *Wish You Were Here*, p11.

[335]Ibid, p12.

[336]Ibid.

[337]Ibid.

[338]Ibid.

[339]'Holiday Snaps' in *Wish You Were Here*, p26.

[340]Ibid, p21. The sequence was published by Windows (a Liverpool poetry organisation) as a Merseyside Poetry Minibook. The PDF is available from the Windows website: http://www.windowsproject.net/publish/minibooks/MPMS29.pdf

[341]'Holiday Snaps' in *Wish You Were Here*, p22.

[342]Ibid.

[343]'Holiday Snaps' in *Wish You Were Here*, p23.

[344]Ibid, p23.

[345]Ibid, p24.

[346]Ibid, p26. The song in question is 'I Want to Know What Love Is' by the

American band, Foreigner. It was a number 1 hit in the UK and the USA in January and February 1985 respectively.

[347]'Holiday Snaps' in *Wish You Were Here*, pp25-26.

[348]Ibid, p26.

[349]'Morning, Liverpool 8' in *Wish You Were Here*, p32; Phil Bowen, *A Gallery to Play To*, p150.

[350]'Morning, Liverpool 8' in *Wish You Were Here*, p32.

[351]Huskisson died after being struck on the inaugural railway journey by Stephenson's 'Rocket' between Liverpool and Manchester on 15 September 1830.

[352]'Wish You Were Here' in *Wish You Were Here*, p37.

[353]'Poem for Roger McGough' in *Selected and Unpublished Poems 1965-2000*, p212.

[354]Roger McGough, 'Vinegar' in *The Mersey Sound*, p81.

[355]'Wish You Were Here' in *Wish You Were Here*, p37.

[356]'Visiting Writer' in *Wish You Were Here*, p40.

[357]Ibid.

[358]William Carlos Williams, *The Wedge* in *Selected Essays of William Carlos Williams* (New York: New Directions, 1969), p256.

[359]Peter Davies, Nicholas Horsfield Obituary, *Independent*, Monday 13 June 2005. Accessed 15 August 2016.

[360]Brian Morley, Nicholas Horsfield Obituary, *Guardian*, Monday 27 June 2005. Accessed 15 August 2016.

[361]Henri and Horsfield were both friends of John Willett (who'd written *Art in a City* in 1967) and both stayed regularly with Willett in a small village near Dieppe.

[362]'Four Studies of Dieppe' in *Wish You Were Here*, p41.

[363]'The Bell' in *Wish You Were Here*, p43.

[364]Ibid.

[365]Ibid.

[366]Ibid.

[367]'For Joyce' in *Wish You Were Here*, p48.

[368]Ibid.

[369]For more about the painting see *Adrian Henri: Paintings 1953-1998*, p114.

[370]Adrian Henri in *Adrian Henri: Paintings 1953-1998*, p108. I can remember clearly both the exhibition in Orrell Park and seeing 'Rapefield' in Bootle Library. The painting is, at the time of writing, currently housed in the Hope St. Hotel in Liverpool city centre.

[371]www.bloodaxebooks.com [accessed 19 August 2016].

[372]The University of Liverpool, The Papers of Adrian Henri, Henri 7/3/19

[373]Other versions of the song were recorded by The Rolling Stones, and more recently, by the likes of Sheryl Crowe and Florence and the Machine. The title 'Not Fade Away' features also as a title for a 1987 novel by American author Jim Dodge.

[374]Rear cover blurb of *Not Fade Away* (Newcastle Upon Tyne: Bloodaxe Books, 1994).

[375]Ibid.

[376]'A Portrait of the Artist' in *Not Fade Away*, p10.

[377]Ibid.

[378]'A Portrait of the Artist' in *Not Fade Away*, p10.

[379]Ibid, p11.

[380]'Honeysuckle, Butterfly, Rose' in *Not Fade Away*, p13.

[381]See http://www.sothebys.com/en/auctions/ecatalogue/2014/british-irish-

art-l14133/lot.8.html <accessed 22 August 2016> The painting itself, is part of the collection of the Russell-Cotes Art Gallery and Museum in Bournemouth. In December 2014, a signed watercolour of the painting was auctioned at Sotheby's and sold for £2,882,500.

[382]'Honeysuckle, Butterfly, Rose' in *Not Fade Away*, p13.

[383]The Rossetti Archive <www.rossettiarchive.org> is a valuable resource.

[384]Catherine Marcangeli, who did her MA on Rossetti, remembers discussing this picture with Henri, 'I was interested in the conflicting symbols in the picture: a halo (that links her to Mary or other pure women), the butterflies (symbol of the soul), the apple (Eve and Venus), the dart (Venus and Cupid), etc. That's what Adrian's poem is partly about, the fact that we're not sure who she is – gentle and pure one minute, fatale the next.' Email to the author, 18 November 2017.

[385]'Honeysuckle, Butterfly, Rose' in *Not Fade Away*, p13.

[386]Ibid.

[387]'Blue for Slim' in *Not Fade Away*, p18.

[388]John Willett, *Art in a City* (Liverpool: Liverpool University Press, 2007).

[389]Phil Bowen, *A Gallery to Play To*, p51.

[390]'Souvenirs' in *Not Fade Away*, p24.

[391]Ibid. Catherine Marcangeli remembers the occasion well: 'We'd driven to Etretat to see the cliffs that Monet had painted but it rained so hard that we couldn't get out of the car – we just sat there, peering at the cliffs through the driving rain and the movement of the windscreen wipers!' Email to the author, 18 November, 2017.

[392]'Souvenirs' in *Not Fade Away*, p24.

[393]Ibid.

[394]'Death Valley' in *Not Fade Away*, p25.

[395]'Souvenirs' in *Not Fade Away*, p24. Catherine Marcangeli remembers Henri pronouncing this correctly as 'Mitsubishi' when giving readings. It must be a typo in the text.

[396]'Impressions d'Afrique' in *Not Fade Away*, p27.

[397]Ibid.

[398]Ibid.

[399]For more about Hawad and Zinsou, the other poet mentioned in Henri's poem, see Richard J. Gray II, *Francophone African Poetry and Drama: A Cultural History since the 1960s* (North Carolina: McFarland and Company, 2014).

[400]'Impressions d'Afrique' in *Not Fade Away*, p27.

[401]'Hello Adrian' from *Tonight at Noon and Other Poems* in *Collected Poems*, pp83-84.

[402]'Impressions d'Afrique' in *Not Fade Away*, p27.

[403]Ibid.

[404]'Impressions d'Afrique' in *Not Fade Away*, p28.

[405]Catherine Marcangeli remembers Henri producing a series of paintings on that trip. Email to author, 18 November 2017.

[406]'From an Antique Land' in *Not Fade Away*, p32.

[407]Ibid, p33.

[408]'From an Antique Land' in *Not Fade Away*, p33.

[409]William Carlos Williams, 'The Red Wheelbarrow' in *The Collected Poems of William Carlos Williams: Volume I 1909-1939* (New York: New Directions, 1986), p224; Adrian Henri, 'The Cerise Swimsuit' in *Not Fade Away*, p37.

[410]Henri would quote the Williams poem before reading 'The Cerise Swimsuit'. Catherine Marcangeli email to the author, 18 November 2017.

[411]The University of Liverpool, The Papers of Adrian Henri, Henri 1/1/43

[412]Adrian Henri, 'Skyline With Cerise Swimsuit, California' in *Adrian Henri: Paintings 1953-1998*, p116.

[413]'Thicket' in *Not Fade Away*, p39.

[414]Ibid.

[415]Ibid.

[416]'Oxford, Sunday, Rain' in *Not Fade Away*, p43.

[417]Ibid.

[418]'Look, Stranger ... ' in *Not Fade Away*, p46.

[419]'Young Man on a Train, 1 May 1990' in *Not Fade Away*, p46.

[420]'Young Man on a Train, 1 May 1990' in *Not Fade Away*, p46.

[421]'Fin de Vacances' in *Not Fade Away*, p48.

[422]Ibid.

[423]For more about Dryden and the poem see St John's College, Cambridge University's library pages. <http://www.joh.cam.ac.uk/john-dryden-annus-mirabilis-1666> site accessed 20 July 2017.

[424]Philip Larkin, 'Annus Mirabilis' in *Collected Poems* (London: Faber and Faber, 1988), p167; 'Annus Mirabilis' in *Not Fade Away*, p57.

[425]Ibid.

[426]'Annus Mirabilis' in *Not Fade Away*, p57.

[427]Ibid.

[428]Neil Kinnock read the poem at the Labour Party Conference that year, later sending Henri a big bunch of red roses as a thank you. Email from Catherine Marcangeli to the author, 18 November 2017.

[429]The Labour Party Manifesto, 1992; 'It's Time to Get Britain Working Again'. Accessed at <http://www.politicsresources.net/area/uk/man/lab92.htm> 20 October 2016

[430]T.S. Eliot, 'The Journey of the Magi' in *Collected Poems,* eds, Christopher Ricks and Jim McCue (London: Faber and Faber, 2015), p101.

[431]Adrian Henri, 'Winter Ending' in *Not Fade Away*, p62.

[432]Ibid.

[433]Ibid.

5

LAST POEMS

Liverpool Accents: Seven Poets and a City (1996)
and *Selected and Unpublished* (2007)

HENRI'S NEXT MAJOR POETRY PUBLICATION CAME in the form of an appearance in the anthology *Liverpool Accents: Seven Poets and a City* published by Liverpool University Press in 1996. The book was edited by Peter Robinson and Henri's involvement was major. The book also featured Elaine Feinstein, Grevel Lindop, Jamie McKendrick, Deryn Rees-Jones, Peter Robinson and Matt Simpson. Henri provided the cover image, a reproduction of 'Esmedune 2000', a mural commissioned by the Royal Liverpool Hospital. Peter Robinson's original preference for the cover was Henri's Hillsborough tribute painting from 1989, 'Flowers for Liverpool'. In a letter dated 29 September 1995 Robinson notes that the idea was received negatively by those to whom he had suggested it.[434] The book was published on the 1 July 1996. It was the last significant appearance of Henri's poetry published during his lifetime.

Henri's selection of eleven poems stemmed back to his debut collection, *Tonight at Noon* ('Liverpool 8'), *City Hedges* ('from *Wasteland*') and *Wish You Were Here* ('Liverpool Poems' and 'The

Bell'). There were also seven, then unpublished, poems. Of these, 'Love in Blackpool' and 'Love in Southport' would later appear in *Selected and Unpublished* published by Liverpool University Press in 2007. As noted in chapter one, what is interesting about the format of *Liverpool Accents* is the introductory statements given by the poets. Henri foregrounds the influence that the city of Liverpool played on his practice as a poet. This statement of poetics gives us an insight into Henri's relationships with the city and with music. As Henri points: 'music has always provided a context for poetry for me, both before and after the event.'[435]

The first selection of Henri's work in *Liverpool Accents* is gathered from *Lowlands Away*, a commission from the Royal Liverpool Philharmonic Orchestra in the form of a collaboration with composer Richard Gordon-Smith. The commission was a piece for soloists, chorus and orchestra and premiered at the Liverpool Philharmonic Hall on 27 April 1996. As Henri explains:

> The [piece] tells the story of the loss at sea of the composer's great-grandfather, the Captain of the Thames and Medway barge *Cynthia* in 1896, and of his last message to his wife, cast into the sea in a bottle and subsequently retrieved and forwarded to her.[436]

It is worth mentioning that the title of the piece stems from a sea shanty and the poems, to an extent, reflect this. Perhaps the most poignant poem is 'Message', which retells the story of the message that eventually found its way to Richard Gordon-Smith's great-grandmother. The poem begins by foregrounding and later repeating a simple four-line stanza:

> A message in a bottle
> entrusted to the sea
> lost in the vague play
> of the waves.[437]

The poem then cites the message from the captain, in its entirety before returning to an extended version of the opening stanza building on the imagery of the sea:

> [...] seen once more,
> then lost from sight
> between sky and shore.[438]

'Oyster' continues the imagery of the sea and the central theme of the selection with the opening lines: 'a message in a bottle/fruit of the womb of the sea [...]'.[439] The strongest poem is the final selection, 'Ballad of the Thames and Medway Barges'. Reminiscent of Henri's early poems such as 'Me' and his blues poems, the poem uses place names, company names and the names of barges in a rhythmic and alphabeticised mode. What is interesting is that the final lines of each of the twelve stanzas, can be read as an individual poem. If we look at the opening two stanzas we can see this pattern developing:

> Aidie Ailsa Agnes Mary
> Abergavenny Alice Ash
> Asphodel Atlantic Atlas
> Beyond the bay where breakers splash
>
> Barbara Jean and British Lion
> British Oak and British King
> Bluebell Bessie Hart and Blackfriars
> Lost to sight where mermaids sing[440]

This technique hints at the ballad mode within the poem, by its strong rhyme, that ends with the final two stanzas repeating a simple concluding line: 'folded in the harbour's care.'[441]

Henri notes the possible difficulties of writing about an 'historical event that took place on the opposite side of the country' yet he explains that because of his location in Liverpool 'seeing the Mersey at the foot of the hill I live on [it is impossible] not to relate the story of Captain Gentry and his ship to the lives and tragedies of Liverpool's mariners over the centuries.'[442] Again, the poet in the city and the influence of the city on the poet, here, is obvious.

Travel was still a major part of Henri's life in the mid-1990s. Henri started travelling to France regularly as Catherine Marcangeli had moved back there in 1996. Readings had taken place in Milan, Bologna and Rome during 1995, as part of a British Council organised series of readings in places such as Dubai and Rotterdam. Closer to home, Henri had read at the Stamps Wine Bar in Crosby, a few miles north of Liverpool, in February 1997, and later in December of that year. In a letter to Henri, Tony Dash who was Sefton Council's Arts contact at the time, thanked Henri for agreeing to read and noted that his performances would be a great inspiration to younger poets.[443]

Further evidence of Henri's travels, though somewhat more locally, appear in *Liverpool Accents: Seven Poets and a City*, in the form of two love poems, 'Love in Blackpool' and 'Love in Southport'. Blackpool and Southport share the same stretch of coast in the North West of England and in the 1950s were popular tourist destinations. To the people of Liverpool and surrounding towns, both Blackpool and Southport were popular day trip destinations, and to some extent, that remains true today. In the poem 'Love in Blackpool', a fourteen-line single-stanza poem, Henri reverts to familiar subjects: love, travel and humour. The observational style that was apparent throughout his writing career is evident at once with the opening three lines:

> In a famous seaside place
> that's noted for fresh air and not much else tonight,
> the lights from The Tower are lost in the fog[444]

By focusing on a famous landmark (The Tower) and the natural world (fresh air and fog), Henri returns to previously used motifs, such as the integration of the manmade and nature.

The out of season setting with 'shuttered gift shop window [s]' and 'dusty sticks' add to the sense that this is a poem of absence. This is confirmed with the final four lines:

> faded bars of rock
> lettered all through say
> I LOVE YOU. The bitter wind
> has fish and chips on its breath.[445]

In 'Love in Southport' we see that seaside town through a clearer lens. It is daytime and 'Pensioners peer in cafe windows, compare/ the price of a cup of tea.'[446] Again, the natural world makes an appearance in the poem: we have plenty of references to ducks, drakes and black-headed gulls that 'gobble crisps, squabble over discarded chips'.[447] There is a sense of measure within the theme of love in 'Love in Southport'. We can deduce that the poem is addressed to Catherine Marcangeli by the inclusion of lines such as '"Wish you were here" I think, yet again' and 'What will you be doing in NYC tonight?'[448] The repeated motifs of the wind and the sand whispering further allows for a sense of absence.

2007 saw the publication of *Selected and Unpublished* by Liverpool University Press. This lavish edition of work, printed in a medium format, was edited by Marcangeli. Carol Ann Duffy, writing in the blurb, noted that 'the poems glow in their colours afresh'.[449] Duffy also spoke at the book's launch at the Everyman Theatre, which saw a gathering of Henri's friends, family and associates.

'Mantlepiece', a poem that appears in the *Selected and Unpublished*, and was published in the *Adrian Henri: Paintings*

1953-1998 exhibition catalogue, is interesting in that we can locate the writing of the poem to an accurate, particular time. In 1994, Henri was in New York visiting Catherine Marcangeli who was in the city as a Fulbright Scholar. This was published by National Museums and Galleries on Merseyside in 2000, to accompany the exhibition of the same name at Liverpool's Walker Art Gallery.[450] The poem is printed opposite a painting entitled *Thanksgiving Parade, New York City III, 1995*. The poem and its accompanying painting is reminiscent of 'The Entry of Christ Into Liverpool' pairing some thirty years earlier. Henri himself noted that:

> When I first painted the picture someone said that it looked like my *Entry of Christ* and perhaps that is true. Ideas kind of lie around in my head. Doing the *New York* paintings set off a sequence of thought that influenced the later *Day of the Dead* paintings.[451]

The painting is in the typical late (from the 1980s on) Henri style with the foot of the canvas un-primed and painted with writing placed there.[452] The poem, a single stanza with fifteen lines, partially punctuated, is a narrative work which replicates the content and form of the painting. It opens with five lines that indicate the true nature of the poem; it is a Henri love poem:

> Between an Art Nouveau swirl
> of yellow-green glass
> and an embroidered heart
> made by an unknown soldier
> for his sweetheart [...][453]

The 'you' of the poem is clearly Catherine Marcangeli, as she is represented in the painting, and as we know, she was the reason Henri was in New York at that time. This representation is accurate in the painting, and the poem interprets her thus:

[...] you clutch a paper cup of coffee
in gloved hands
brown velvet cap pulled low
shading the resentment.[454]

In the painting Marcangeli has her back to the crowd, indicating that there was perhaps some resentment towards the occasion.[455]

The poem then shifts from a description of 'a team deflates/the giant Snoopy behind you' to

NYPD POLICE LINE DO NOT NOT CROSS[456]

The biggest shift, though, is from the following line, 'between us', which could refer to the police barrier being between the speaker and Marcangeli's representation, or be a link to the final two lines:

On the landing, you are laughing,
your arms full of willowherb.[457]

'Mantlepiece' is an interesting poem not least due to its proximity to 'Thanksgiving Day Parade, New York City III, 1995' in the Walker catalogue, and Henri's comments about the events that inspired it give us a useful perspective: 'It was a particular bleak November day – a dull rather cold rainy day with these garish things floating between the great canyon of the street.[458] However, it is the compositional style that is of particular note: 'I took photographs or rather Catherine took photographs and I selected bits and played around with the elements.' [459] The poem is familiar to earlier work such as 'The Entry of Christ Into Liverpool' with its collage process.

The Walker exhibition guide is useful in providing context for another late important Henri poem, 'The Day of the Dead, Hope Street'. The poem was selected by Catherine Marcangeli for *Selected and Unpublished*.[460] Clearly referencing his own work from the mid-1960s, in the form of 'The Entry of Christ Into Liverpool', 'The Day of the Dead, Hope Street, 1998' (the painting) follows the form of the earlier painting in depicting religious iconography; Liverpool's Metropolitan Cathedral of Christ the King features in the painting (the Cathedral sits at one end of Hope Street, whilst Liverpool's Anglican Cathedral sits at the other end), although the most striking resemblance are the figures located in the painting. The figures in the later painting are interspersed with skeletons, an allusion to the title of the piece. Figures from Henri's 'The Entry of Christ Into Liverpool' also appear in the later work. Joyce Henri and the artist Sam Walsh appear alongside such heroes as Allen Ginsberg and William S. Burroughs. The black cat in both paintings also appears in both poems. In locating the piece in Hope Street, we have the foregrounding of places that were of importance to Henri. The Philharmonic Pub and the Everyman Theatre, where Henri staged many events including the first Happenings in the UK in 1962, and the Casa, an underground after-hours drinking den in the 1980s, is represented, rather tellingly, by a red star. A nice touch by Henri was to include Catherine Marcangeli's father in the painting alongside the Mexican, French tricolour and the Union flags to represent their relationship. Contrary to the figures depicted in 'The Entry of Christ Into Liverpool', all of the people in the painting are dead.

'The Day of the Dead, Hope Street' is similar, not only in content to the earlier poem, 'The Entry of Christ Into Liverpool', but also in length and style. Each poem begins with the quiet of morning building through the crescendo of events towards the quiet of evening contemplation. The poem, which, unlike 'The Entry of Christ Into Liverpool', is regularised by the left-hand margin, and is in nine irregular stanzas. The opening stanza, with a location specific nod to the early poem, sets the scene:

> silence in Hope Street
> silence in stony places
> after the agony in St Luke's Gardens
> silence [461]

The repetition of 'silence' 'after the agony in St Luke's Gardens', which is a place referenced in 'The Entry of Christ Into Liverpool', contrasts with the tone of the following festive stanzas. It is worth noting that St Luke's Gardens is the churchyard of St Luke's Church, which is known locally as 'the bombed-out church' as it was damaged during the Liverpool Blitz of World War II.

An outside narratorial voice announces 'Ladies and Gentlemen/ Señors y Señoras/for one night only/The Simultaneous and Historical Faces of Death!'[462] This again, is reminiscent of the earlier poem, with that particular narratorial voice being consigned to the left-hand margin, while the 'action' of the poem is centred. There is a clear nod to 'The Entry of Christ Into Liverpool' with the appearance of a black cat. The cat appears in both paintings and both poems, here she 'picks her way between the dancers'.[463] Henri was a cat lover and uses the cat to provide a way of subverting the traditional symbol of the black cat bringing bad luck. The poem 'Cat' closes Henri's 1983 collection *Penny Arcade* and the 1986 *Collected Poems.* The poem, as it appears in the *Collected*, comes complete with three sketches/drawings featuring the cat, including the cat highlighted as it appears in the painting of 'The Entry of Christ Into Liverpool' and the book's final page features a full page drawing of Henri holding the cat.[464]

Throughout 'The Day of the Dead in Hope Street', the senses are fully explored. Colour is presented throughout with mentions of 'heaped marigolds scream orange defiance [...] tequila in hand/ bloodred tropical sunset [...] pink and white boas.'[465] Henri updates the setting of the poem/painting by highlighting the use of technology:

> fade in F.X. laughter
> faint boxy sound of cheap guitars
> songs torn from dried-up larynxes[466]

This contrasts with the musical instruments mentioned in 'The Entry of Christ Into Liverpool':

> THE SOUND OF TRUMPETS
> and
> THE MARCHING DRUMS[467]

The implication is that there is a live element to the proceedings, as part of the event itself.

The musicality continues throughout 'The Day of the Dead, Hope Street' which adds not only to the sense of occasion to the poem, but leads to the final, calming stanza. This again, is reminiscent of 'The Entry of Christ Into Liverpool':

> at dusk
> the carnival departs
> hands yellow with the dust of mimosa
> hair braided with crimson carnations
> a trail of bright red petals
> trodden beneath her limping feet
> echoing distant laughter
> along the empty street[468]

The narrative elements of both poems are highlighted by the layout and the linearity of the day's events. They both share a sense of occasion, albeit different events, the musicality and festiveness. There is also an awareness of the poem 'City', with its varying modes of referencing the city.

Another poem from *Selected and Unpublished* that is worth

considering is 'The New, Fast, Automatic Daffodils/Two'. This poem harks back to a poem that was published in both *The Mersey Sound* and *Tonight at Noon*, 'The New, Fast, Automatic Daffodils'. Both poems were deemed important enough for Catherine Marcangeli to include them in *Selected and Unpublished*. If we look first to the original poem, Henri points to his writing mode by giving the poem an epigraph: 'New variation on Wordsworth's "Daffodils"' and a footnote: 'cut-up of Wordsworth's poem plus Dutch motor-car leaflet'.[469] Here Henri is evidencing the influence of William S. Burroughs who, along with Brion Gysin, pioneered the cut-up methodology in Paris in the late 1950s. The poem reads like an early Henri poem with its mixed use of capital letters and layout:

> I wandered lonely as
> THE NEW, FAST DAFFODIL
>   FULLY AUTOMATIC
> that floats on high o'er vales and hills[470]

The humour that greets the reader with the recognisable lines from Wordsworth interrupted by the cut-up element from the car brochure, is reminiscent of Henri's earlier work. The final line of the poem again shows the humour of the poem: 'Travelling by Daffodil you can relax and enjoy every mile of the journey.'[471] This slightly absurdist humour can be traced back to Henri's appreciation of the Alfred Jarry creation Père Ubu. In fact, Catherine Marcangeli chose a 1987 Henri collage, depicting Ubu for the author photograph on the inside cover of *Selected and Unpublished*. Henri's use of Ubu can be seen in earlier artworks such as 'Père Ubu in Liverpool' which shares the title of a poem, and 'Père Ubu on Rhyl Sands'. Henri had this to say about the influence of Ubu on his practice:

Ubu, I think, was meant to personify all the bourgeois vices [...]
One thing I like about him is that despite the fact that he is a monster
in a way, he is also somehow a survivor. [...] I liked the idea of
putting him in Liverpool [...] then I put him in other places and he
crops up in several poems located in Liverpool.[472]

An example of an Ubu poem is 'Père Ubu in Liverpool' which
featured in Henri's debut collection *Tonight at Noon* and *Selected
and Unpublished*. The poem is presented as a short play, with
instructions, songs and a cast list. Henri uses famous locations
around Liverpool such as The Cavern, Lewis's department store
and the Cathedral. The cast includes Ubu, a group of Mods and a
Liverpool bird. Though dated, this terminology for a woman, seems
somehow appropriate for the poem due to its use at the time:

> *Ubu*: Ah. And that is no doubt a statue of Mr Lewis?
> *Bird*: (pointing upward and giggling):
> What – *dat?* No. Dat's 'Scouse'.[473]

Henri here is referring to the naked sculpture that is located on
the Lewis's department store. The sculpture by Sir Jacob Epstein,
called 'Liverpool Resurgent', is of a naked man on the bow of a
ship, known locally as 'Dickie' Lewis. It was used by locals as a
meeting place. It is interesting to note that Ubu and his creator,
Alfred Jarry, appear in the painting 'The Entry of Christ into
Liverpool' and Jarry is namechecked in the poem of the same title.

In the second version of the 'The New, Fast, Automatic Daffodils'
poem, 'The New, Fast, Automatic Daffodils/Two', Henri resists the
urge to replicate the form and technique of the earlier poem. Rather,
the poem plays with extant lines in a repetitious mode and adheres
to a strict rhyme scheme, as the opening stanza shows:

> I wandered lonely as a lonely cloud
> I wandered lonely as a lonely cloud

> I wandered lonely through the lonely crowd
> an all-at-once, a one-time only crowd
> a host, a cloud of roots that clutch
> a host, a crowd of looks that touch
> that floats on high o'er vales and hills
> that floats on, high on booze and pills
> as stoned and lonely as the daffodils.[474]

The poem is reminiscent of earlier Henri blues poems, which riff on lines and rhythm and rhyme, though Henri is attempting to update the form, by aping the form of the emerging rap culture.[475] The reference to an earlier version of a poem is similar in many ways to Henri's method with poems/paintings such as 'The Entry of Christ Into Liverpool'. The use of words like 'high' and 'stoned' indicate the then contemporary nature of the poem (its date of composition is unknown).

Two poems with dedicatees feature in the unpublished selection of *Selected and Unpublished*: 'A Landscape for Adrian', dedicated to Adrian Mitchell on the occasion of his 65th birthday and 'Eco-Poem', dedicated to Roger McGough. 'A Landscape for Adrian' has an epigraph from a Mitchell poem, 'Life is a Walk Across a Field': ' ... *a walk across a field/of buttercups and landmines*'.[476] The poem is, in many ways, typical of Henri's work with images of nature, urbanisation and the passing of time. The opening lines of the twelve-lined, single-stanza poem encapsulates what is to follow, 'To walk ten years on/find the piteous earth torn by landmines'. The sense of nature being all powerful is evident: 'poppyseeds await patient decades/to spurt bloodred across forgotten battlefields'. The compound words bring to mind early Henri poems and the image of the reclamation of nature is a familiar trait, as 'grass picks its quiet way/through the tarmac of out-of-town hypermarkets'.[477]

'Eco-Poem' takes us back to *The Mersey Sound*. Henri returns to the humour that graced the early work, in particular, 'Poem for Roger McGough' which appears in the 'Short Poems' section of *The Mersey Sound*.[478]

A further example from 'Short Poems' that typifies the mode of the Henri short poem, is 'Cat Poem'. Cats, as noted above, feature heavily in Henri's art and poetry. 'Cat Poem' trades on the humour in evidence in much of the early work:

> You're black and sleek and beautiful
> What a pity your best friends won't tell you
> Your breath smells of Kit-E-Kat[479]

This mix of human and animal behaviours combined with anthropomorphizing the cat, is evidence of a considered mode of composition, rather than merely trading solely on humour.

'Eco-Poem' plays with the notion of what an 'Eco-Poem' can be. Again, it is short and playful:

> 'I'm saving energy'
> he said
> not switching off the light.[480]

The irony here, of course, is the fact that the poem's speaker is, in fact, saving energy, possibly his own energy, by not moving to switch off the light, which is at the cost of the environment.

For *Selected and Unpublished* Catherine Marcangeli divided the poetry into three thematic sections, with the second and third sections divided further into two sections. The unpublished work is placed at the end of each section. The poems aren't placed in chronological order (though they are within each section). The themes of each section are pretty evident. Part I is titled 'Love Is' after the poem of the same name, and consists of Henri's love poems. Part II, 'Home and Away', is divided into two sections,

'Metropolis' and 'Wish You Were Here', the former after a poem, and the latter after Henri's 1990 collection.

Each section and associated part of the book is introduced by associates and friends of Henri: Brian Patten, Roger McGough, Willy Russell and Adrian Mitchell. The foreword is by Henri's former girlfriend, Carol Ann Duffy. Perhaps the most interesting aspect of the book is the unpublished translations that appear. 1965 translations of French poets Alain Bosquet and Jacques Prévert appear alongside 1995 translations of Dutch writer Bert Schierbeek and 1996 translations of South African painter and poet, Breyten Breytenbach.[481] We can only guess at Henri's mode of translation, as, though he knew some French, it is unclear whether he knew Dutch, but if we look to the Prévert translation, we can see the influence on Henri's poetics. In an interview with Catherine Marcangeli, she mentioned the influence of Prévert on Henri:

> Prévert of course, if you're looking at the city, he's the major influence really. He was the reason we got talking in the first place. The first time I saw Adrian read was in early 1986, and when we talked the first thing I asked was whether he had heard of Prévert, because his work reminded me of him, and he said 'Yeah' and I said, thought so! Prévert is largely about the city and the poetry of the city and the flea markets [like the Surrealists]. For Adrian in a way, the city is the everyday and the country is the eternal.[482]

Prévert is best known as the author of *Paroles*. The translation by Lawrence Ferlinghetti that appeared through his City Lights publishing house in 1958, is one of the company's best sellers and has remained in print since its original publication date. Prévert is still studied in France and his quiet observational style, mixed with surrealism is revered. *Paroles* was listed by the French newspaper, *Le Monde*, as one of the books of the millennium.[483]

Prévert's 'What Were You Thinking About?' is a thirteen-line, two-stanza poem that could easily have been placed in Henri's selection for *The Mersey Sound* or his debut collection *Tonight at Noon*. The opening stanza, with its surreal nature akin to Henri's own 'Tonight at Noon', plays with the reader's expectations with its ambiguity:

Dressed and then dressed again
what were you thinking about
undressed[484]

The second longer stanza continues with the surreal tone and playfulness, opening with two contrasting images of the narrator and a shared domestic locale: 'I left my mink in the hallway/and we went into the desert' which leads to the repeated and inverted lines of 'We lived on love and cold water/we loved each other in our poverty' and later in the poem, 'We loved each other in our poverty/ we lived on love and cold water'[485] These central lines are followed by 'we even ate our dirty linen in public/and on the black sand tablecloth/the sunlight spread its golden dishes' and 'my body your freehold property' respectively. This allows for the emphasis to be placed on love above all else and the surrealism to be brought into the mix.

A later translation of Bert Schierbeek's poem, 'We Won't Forget That', notes that it is 'From the Dutch of, and in memory of Bert Schierbeek'.[486] Schierbeek died in 1996. Famed for his 'composition novels', Schierbeek would also be active in CoBrA, the avant-garde movement, that took its name from the home cities of its members: Copenhagen, Brussels and Amsterdam.[487] The poem, eleven lines long and in a single stanza, plays again with repetition and captures the essences of both poets with their mix of surrealism and humour. Henri's translation plays with two voices, mixing the 'I' and the 'We' around the central question of the title:

> we won't forget that
> that we laughed, laughed that
> much I'll never forget that
> that we laughed that much, will we?[488]

The comma is the only piece of punctuation in the poem apart from the question mark that follows. Henri uses enjambment interestingly, breaking the word 'because' across two lines as 'be/cause'. This is in contrast to the use of compound words that Henri employed particularly in the early work. The word 'laughter' appears in this short poem seven times, and the word 'forget', six times. The total word count of the poem is sixty-one words. As a poem *in memoriam*, it focuses primarily on reminiscing and laughter, while adhering to Schierbeek's avant-garde aesthetic by its use of repetition.[489]

Another poem published in *Liverpool Accents*, but omitted from *Selected and Unpublished*, and which needs consideration is 'Mr Punch Speaks'. The poem, subtitled 'a Modern Olympia', is footnoted 'after Arthur Ballard's "Punch and His Judy", Atkinson Art Gallery, Southport'.[490] Author Peter Davies paints Henri's relationship with Ballard as problematic. Ballard was a teacher at the Liverpool College of Art, while Henri had taught there in the early 1960s. Seen as one of the old guard, Davies argues that Ballard was resistant to the experimental ethos of the younger Art College staff such as Henri. This wasn't the case. Schooled in an abstract tradition, Davies alleges that Ballard found it difficult managing a career at the College, raising a family and keeping pace with the changes afoot in the art world. However, as Catherine Marcangeli notes:

> Ballard had been very experimental himself, in a School of Paris style. The younger painters admired the fact that Arthur had lived and worked in Paris with the likes of Serge Poliakoff. The artists in Liverpool may have disagreed on artistic matters, but they respected each other.[491]

Ballard would later have a brush with fame after the deaths of his former students Stuart Sutcliffe and John Lennon. Sutcliffe would leave the fledgling band, The Beatles, some say at Ballard's suggestion, to focus on painting, while Lennon went on to worldwide fame with the band and his solo career until his untimely death in 1980, aged 40.[492]

Henri was, in the early 1960s, at the forefront of a new wave of artistic experimentation. Henri said that Ballard was 'totally out of sympathy' with what they [Don McKinlay, Maurice Cockrill and Sam Walsh] were doing.[493] 'But he could see that it was good, and he could see it was different and it was original.'[494] There seems to have been a little thawing in the hostility on Henri's part, perhaps following Ballard's death in 1994.[495] 'Mr Punch Speaks' is an ekphrastic poem continuing the seaside themes of 'Love in Blackpool' and 'Love in Southport'. The traditional characters of Punch & Judy, the puppets that play in seaside resorts across the UK, appear in the poem as a literal representation of Ballard's painting. In another link to the seaside resort section of poems in *Liverpool Accents*, Ballard's painting is housed in the permanent collection of Southport's Atkinson art gallery. The painting, part of a series featuring the Punch and Judy characters as human forms, features a naked couple on a bed, with flowers in the foreground, and the male figure pointing towards the viewer from the centre of the canvas.

The poem opens in a threatening tone, slightly passive-aggressive and suitably accusatory and undercut with a hint of humour:

> She's mine Don't think
> I haven't seen you looking at her,
> sunshine [...][496]

As if to heighten the control the male has over the female, he notes that 'I made her,/just like Galatea. One day she'll be old, like me'.[497] Galatea here perhaps refers to both of the Greek mythological definitions; a name meaning 'she who is milk white' and the name of a woman who prayed for her daughter to be turned into a son, Leucippus. This conversational tone continues throughout the poem. The threats and aggression appear again, though once again undercut with humour:

> All you see is this one: young,
> warm, desirable. Watch it. I've seen
> that look in pubs and clubs.[498]

Henri uses slant rhyme to good effect in the lines: 'Eyes/out on stalks. Don't think I haven't heard the talk'[499] maintaining the menace of the speaker's voice. The final part of the poem brings the speaker close to the observer of the painting and the reader of the poem. Drawing on the man who voices the poem, we again are met with the by now familiar theme of hostility and humour:

> And now, in this gallery,
> there's you. Just heed the pointing finger,
> don't linger too long. And remember:
> keep your eyes to yourself.[500]

Much of 1996 and 1997 was taken up with Henri curating an exhibition in Liverpool. Henri was also appointed artist/facilitator in residence at the 150 Years Celebration of Public Health in the city and managed also to fit in a 30th anniversary tour of *The Mersey Sound* with Brian Patten and Roger McGough, alongside trips to the Edinburgh Festival and to Argentina. Henri took his role seriously as artist/facilitator in residence. He worked closely with Professor John Ashton, who was at that time North West Regional Director of Health and Regional Medical Officer, and the idea for an exhibition of art to celebrate Dr William Henry Duncan of Liverpool, who was the UK's first Medical Officer of Health, came about through this close relationship. Henri's association with Ashton stemmed back to the mural 'Esmedune 2000' that Henri had painted at the Royal Liverpool Hospital in 1993. It was Ashton who had initiated the idea of artwork in hospital waiting areas. In a paper published in the *Journal of Epidemiology and Community Health* titled 'The Death of an Artist: Adrian Henri 1932-2000', he highlights the relationship between himself and Henri:

> At the first Healthy Cities conference, held in Lisbon in 1986, I presented a paper – 'Esmedune 2000' – which sought to draw together a strategic vision for a future, regenerated Liverpool based on a coalescence of community initiatives and more formal, large scale public works projects.[501]

Henri responded to this by writing a poem called 'City 2000' that Ashton uses in his article. At the time of writing, the poem remains uncollected. Interestingly, Henri alludes to poetry as a visual device and perhaps is referencing his painting:

> The night
> written in dripping white
> on a railway wall
> 'Swarming city, city full of dreams' [502]

Here Henri points us to his literary inheritance with the line ('Swarming city, city full of dreams', from Charles Baudelaire's poem 'The Seven Old Men'.)[503] It is interesting to note that Henri also uses the line in the introduction text to his long poem 'City', but does not credit Baudelaire; similarly the quote appears as a subtitle to Henri's introductory essay in the Peter Robinson edited collection *Liverpool Accents: Seven Poets and a City*.[504] 'City 2000' is reverential in tone with allusions to how the city is 'no longer an

embarrassment'. Perhaps the strongest lines are saved for the end
of the poem; with the final rhyme providing a cliché of finality:

> This city
> is your mother
> and your lover
> She is your first thought
> and your last
> She is your future and your past[505]

Ashton also cites another poem yet to be collected, 'Ode to Dr
Duncan'. The poem, telling a narrative is clearly a companion to
the artwork 'Dr Duncan in Seel Street' that Henri contributed to
the exhibition he curated in 1997.[506] The poem begins with an
appropriate quotation from Macbeth:

> ' ... this Duncan
> Hath borne his faculties so meek, hath been
> So clear in his great efforts, that his virtues
> Will plead like angels ... '
>
> – Shakespeare, Macbeth

The opening stanza is again reminiscent of a Henri blues poem,
its rhythm and rhyme conforming to reader expectation:

> As I was a-walking down Paradise Street
> a figure in black I happened to meet
> a smile on his face instead of a frown
> a ghost walks the streets of Liverpool Town[507]

The form of the poem, with its italicised references to Liverpool
streets, place names and the river, has a certain musicality, like the
much earlier 'Blues' poems, certainly with the repetition of the
opening stanza as the penultimate stanza. Dr Duncan is firmly
located in modern day Liverpool, with its 'cracked pavements,/
burst-open black bags, polystyrene food-trays,/drifts of chip-

papers,/abandoned copies of THE BIG ISSUE.'[508] This positioning of
Dr Duncan in the city matches the aforementioned painting of Dr
Duncan in the city's Seel Street:

> Turning on impulse to home, he walks down Seel Street;
> dazed by the neon lure of nightclubs,
> he does not notice the familiar figures
> huddled on the steps of the Mission of Charity.[509]

Seel Street in the city centre is important, as Dr Duncan was
born in number 106, which is now part of the Liverpool nightclub
The Blue Angel. Henri also points to the Mission of Charity on
Seel Street. This charity, that offers help to the city's homeless, sold
its garden to developers who built a new city square. The strength
of the poem is in the defamiliarization of locating Duncan in
modern Liverpool with his concerns manifesting due to his position
as Medical Officer of Health.

The Dr Duncan Art Show, curated by Henri in association with
Maggi Morris of the Duncan Society took place in the former
Museum of Liverpool Life on the banks of the Mersey. The
exhibition ran from 12 December 1997 until 15 March 1998. There
were fifteen artists represented showing work in various mediums
responding to what public health meant to them.

Henri's own health was of concern during mid-1998. In May he
had a heart pacemaker fitted. Prior to this, the usual Henri touring
and reading activities took place, including trips to Galway, and
Fowey in Cornwall, for appearances at literature festivals. 1998 also
saw the publication of a selected poems for children, *The World's
Your Lobster*, and a new collection of children's poetry, *Robocat*,
both published by Bloomsbury Children's Books.

Henri's health further deteriorated when in June 1998 he suffered
heart failure and was hospitalised – this, unsurprisingly, had an

effect on his creative output. While there were two solo exhibitions of his art in Liverpool and Stockport, and group exhibitions in Birmingham and Cologne, alongside an exhibition with his friend, Don McKinlay, he wrote and published little poetry after this time, aside from the children's poetry books.

It is interesting to note that by the late 1990s all three of 'The Mersey Poets' had had successful alternative writing careers, writing for children. McGough had published six collections for children and co-edited with Graham Dean, *Strictly Private: Anthology of Poetry* published by Puffin Teenage Poetry. Brian Patten had published titles such as *Gargling with Jelly*, published by Puffin in 2003 and had edited *The Puffin Book of 20th-Century Children's Verse*, with Michael Foreman. With McGough, Patten had written *The Monster's Guide to Choosing a Pet* published by Puffin Poetry in 2005.

1999 started badly. Henri had a heart by-pass operation in January. Despite the procedure being deemed a success, in February, after a massive stroke, Henri was left paralysed. The prognosis was dire. It was doubtful that Henri would walk or talk again. Marcangeli was determined to help aid Henri to recover, and her determination was matched by Henri's will power to make progress after such a devastating turn of events. The task of preparing for the *Adrian Henri; Paintings 1953-1998* Exhibition at Liverpool's Walker Art Gallery had been in hand when Henri was taken ill. His hospitalisation was to last over six months. He did learn to talk and walk again, and to write and paint again.

Another example of Henri's poetics is to be found in *Selected and Unpublished*. The final section of the book, 'If You Weren't You … ', is split into two parts. 'Look, Stranger', the second part, begins with a statement from Henri himself. It gives us a glimpse into Henri's creative practice throughout his career, but perhaps these words seem rather more prescient when we consider the final poems:

> One thing I think is interesting about working today is a sort of awareness about how personal content can go into a work of art and not violate its universal validity.[510]

The unique selling point of *Selected and Unpublished* is the arrangement of Henri's poetry alongside a selection of his artwork. The reproduction of the artwork is rather substandard compared to the catalogue for the Walker exhibition. However, it is the unpublished work that is to be cherished. If we consider that Henri's previous collection, *Not Fade Away*, was published by Bloodaxe in 1994, and is out of print, *Selected and Unpublished* is a valuable book.[511]

'The Image' is an unpublished poem gathered in the 'Look, Stranger' section of the book with a mournful, reflective tone that is indicative of the final Henri poems. It is unpunctuated until a full stop appears on the final line. The opening of the poem refers to the image of the title as 'the dark tunnel/with nightmare orange lights' and 'the voice on the radio/saying there is a change to the advertised programme.'[512] The opening line prepares the reader for what is essentially a rather bleak poem that relies on a few sparse colourful images to lighten the impact:

> It is the sound of rain on cellophane
> round pink and white carnations [...]
> It is a wreath of white plastic chrysanthemums
> in a Liverpool shop window [...][513]

Movement and simplicity are in evidence alongside religious imagery:

> It is the patient shuffling of lines of umbrellas
> it is a child's praying hands
> against a blue school sweatshirt [...][514]

The image of 'patient' shuffling offers a sense of resignation. We can determine that this is a later Henri poem, (despite the mention of plastic flowers and namechecking Liverpool), as schoolchildren only started wearing branded school uniform sweatshirts relatively recently.[515] The image here, of a child praying, offers the reader the chance to return to childhood, school assemblies and more innocent times, perhaps. In the final six lines of the poem, the poem makes reference to a camera, and the fact that the mechanical (in the form of the camera) is located outside of the poem itself:

> In the endless clicking of shutters
> it is the final image
> That you will not see
> That no one can take away from you
> It is the minute's silence
> at the end of the poem.[516]

The use of capitalization of the word 'That' in succeeding lines indicates a possible pause and it feels as though there is a definite shift before the final two lines, as silence 'at the end of the poem' again returns us to a sense of reflective calm, and contemplation. 'The Image' uses the skilled eye of the artist to match the crafting of words from a poet towards the end of his life. The poem has a considered feel to it. Henri, like most poets, was able to write for an occasion.[517]

One example of such a poem, appears not in print, but exists in a frame at Liverpool John Moores University (LJMU). LJMU was the former Liverpool Polytechnic that was granted University status in 1992. It is a city-centre university and as such the opportunity to build and expand was limited. In 1994 however, on Upper Duke Street in Liverpool, around the corner from Henri's Mount Street home, LJMU opened the Dean Walters building. Named after Derrick Walters, Dean of Liverpool's Anglican Cathedral from 1983 until his death in 2000, the mighty building casts its shadows onto Upper Duke Street. Walters was instrumental in the regeneration of the Upper Duke Street area that housed the building that bore his name. The building was sold by LJMU in 2014 for £2,300,000. Twenty years previously, in 1994, Henri had penned the poem 'The Poem Has Gone to University', in honour of the opening of the building.

The poem, which is housed in an office in LJMU's new Clarence Street Redmonds Building, is a clever play on poetic form and uses some familiar Henri techniques. If we look at the opening stanza of five we can see comparisons with 'The Image':

> It will learn to be
> a dramatic monologue,
> with suitable lighting
> and a well-designed set.[518]

The poem continues to trade on the poetry and form relationship as the third stanza cleverly shows, replicating the form it refers to:

> It will learn to be
> a seventeen-syllable
> Japanese verse

Of course, this is the form of the Haiku, written in seventeen syllables, with the allusion to the seasons.

Similarly, the fourth stanza continues this playfulness with 'attracted to alliteration, with alacrity' and the final stanza 'finishes with/the heroic couplet/of a First Class Degree.' Though not one of the strongest of Henri's later poems, it is reminiscent of the defamiliarising effect of earlier work such as 'Tonight at Noon' and 'Mrs Albion, You've Got a Lovely Daughter'.

'The Hours of the Insomniac' appears in the 'Look, Stranger' part of *Selected and Unpublished*. This long poem, which takes up three and a half pages in nineteen stanzas, of varying lengths, traces the long night that the insomniac faces. It begins with an epigraph from Berholt Brecht's 'The First Psalm': 'How terrifying is the night,/ the convex face of the black land.'[519] The poem continues the Brechtian link with its opening italicised line of '*um Mitternacht*' (at Midnight) and takes the reader back to the childhood image of the night terrors with 'afraid of the dark forest/huddled in the dark for comfort/switch on the light/on the unnecessary landing.'[520] We are, however, made aware that the poem is not dealing with childhood and those fears of the dark. The second stanza begins with the speaker's voice 'picking at the scar-tissue of memory/shades of abandoned projects' and 'phonecalls not made/poems unwritten'.[521] This sense of regretful wakefulness recurs throughout the rest of the stanza:

> dusty folders exhumed
> then reinterred mingle
> with cries of night club goers
> howl of car alarms
> crunch or past daydreams
> the sound of smashed windscreens[522]

Through this repetition of disruptive and destructive images it is easy to assume that Henri is building on the memories of the 1981 'Toxteth' riots that he had written about in poems such as 'Morning, Liverpool 8' and 'Adrian Henri's Talking Toxteth Blues'. The third and fourth stanzas of 'The Hours of the Insomniac' take us out of the concrete world of the insomniac and into a dreamy, surreal mode where 'ice-floes piled horizontal/have pushed through the bedroom window' and snowflakes 'settle on the dark green sheets/melt on your warm body'. The speaker is not alone in the bedroom. The poem then mixes references from popular culture in the form of Great Grimpen Mire, from Arthur Conan Doyle's

The Hound of the Baskervilles, and the contemporary, by referring to the Berlin Wall and 'one casual gesture enough/to call down the waiting Stasi, VoPo,/grey-clad GrePo'.[523] These references to the former German Democratic Republic and the state apparatus used to enforce the wall, are perhaps references to the gulf between sleep and wakefulness, and the striving to overcome the latter.

The timescale of the poem continues from its midnight starting point. In the sixth stanza we are given the time of 'Three o'clock' while the eighth stanza announces that 'in the dark night of the soul/it is always 4 a.m.'[524] We are then re-introduced to the other person located in the poem:

> you wake
> a stranger
> turn away from me
> a stranger
> warm back an ocean away [525]

This allows for a sense of isolation to be brought to the fore. There is a slowing in the pace of the poem and a reflective pause in the next two lines: '5.00/familiar red bedside glow' alluding to the digital display of a clock radio alarm.[526] What follows is a stanza laced with negatives, summing up the mood of the speaker: 'the wrong footpath', 'lost turnings', 'wrong words, lost clothes', 'futile panic' and 'forgotten poems, locked corridors'.[527] Then we are met by another time stamp: '5.05: criminal shadows. Slow march of red digits'.[528] This works particularly well after the fast-paced negatives of the previous stanza.

The combination of the reintroduction of the other person who inhabits the poem alongside time, is a signifier that the poem is heading towards its end:

> your phantom smell beneath the bedclothes

> real as the half-dreamt knocking
>   on the 6.00 a.m. door[529]

A further reference to the city appears in the penultimate stanza with 'dawn chorus of police sirens/keyboard-chatter of rain'.[530] This is particularly powerful when we consider the usual dawn chorus is part of the natural order of things and typically associated with wildlife.

The final stanza is preceded by another time stamp: 'Eight o'clock'.[531] We are led towards the realisation that sleep has deserted the poem's speaker and are then met with a final stanza bereft of any sense of relief at the appearance of morning:

> the light
> is the colour of the tears
> that squeeze from beneath
>   your closed eyelids.[532]

The speaker's partner, who has had a non-speaking role in the stretch of night, becomes active, but with tears that produce light. Are we to assume that this is the light of 8.00 a.m?

'The Hours of the Insomniac' is a poem a world away from 'The Poem Has Gone To University'. The frivolity and celebratory nature of 'The Poem Has Gone To University', combined with its educational references, seems distant from the personal nature of the world of the insomniac in the latter poem. What this shows us is the breadth of Henri's poetry, from the seemingly frivolous to the considered and reflective.

In terms of locating some of the last poems Henri produced and which were published in *Selected and Unpublished*, Marcangeli has shown a keen editorial awareness. Situating a poem such as 'Coronary Care Unit' at the end of the opening section of *Selected and Unpublished* titled 'Love Is ... ' raises not only the importance of the poem, but foregrounds the fact that it is a love poem. It is also one of the last poems that Adrian Henri wrote in 1999. Bel Mooney, writing in *The Times Magazine* in January 2000, dates the poem as being written in spring of that year during the six-month hospitalisation that Henri endured.[533] However, this seems unlikely, and it is possible that the poem was completed later in the year. As noted earlier, Henri had two massive strokes in February of 1999.

'Coronary Care Unit' consists of five numbered stanzas. It spans two pages of *Selected and Unpublished*. In many ways it is a difficult poem to read. The poem's subject matter is often painful to navigate.

The poem opens with a familiar Henri motif – nature. Of course, we are aware, courtesy of the title, where we as readers are located. Henri cleverly uses the naturalistic images to contrast the actual location in which the poem is set. The first half of the stanza surreally juxtaposes the natural world with the sterile hospital ward. It is also reminiscent of 'The Hours of the Insomniac' with the quest for sleep over wakefulness:

> 1
> False dawn
> of the desk lamp
> night wind
> from the electric fan
> stirs the leaves in the partition curtains.[534]

We then are placed in the post-slumber wakefulness of 'the real, striped green dawn', where 'they bring back cups of tea/from the water-hole/as we watch from the sheeted savannah.'[535] This clever use of contrasting the morning ritual of tea with the desert's provider of water, hints at the potential life-saving nature of the coronary care unit.

The second stanza shifts the focus to the practicalities of being in a ward or unit, where life is fragile. The opening line announces, in speech marks, 'Cardiac arrest in the coronary care unit'.[536] The voice is unidentified, intimating that it is a loud speaker broadcast, calling for assistance. The nameless 'life next door' that 'flickers beyond the frail curtain' brings home the fine line between life and death; even the curtains are frail.[537] Henri then offers what in another poem might seem comical:

> He asks for his singlet. They've never heard
> the word. 'Cardiac arrest ... '
> Don't they know
> he means a vest?[538]

The hint of humour, alongside a sense of helplessness, is evident in the fact that such an archaic word for vest is being used and not recognised, is reaffirmed by the rhyme of 'arrest' and 'vest', by the child-like rhyme. It also suggests something about the nameless patient: he's old.

The third and fourth stanzas return to the nature motifs evident in the first two stanzas. We have 'Breath distant as sunlit, sheep-filled hills', and 'His last sharp cries/wheel in the air like seagulls'.[539] Henri also returns us to the streets of Liverpool (he was hospitalised in The Royal Liverpool University Hospital, a stone's throw from his studio on Prescott Street) with 'Outside, the terraces, the tower-blocks/cough black night.'[540] The final line is possibly referring to the noises heard in the ward/unit. The atmosphere of the ward is in evidence, 'Lungs strain towards the light./Jagged lines on the monitor. Electric bleeps.'[541] The mix of the personal and the anonymous city appear in the fourth stanza:

> The hollow roar of his chest
> dominates the room
> like the skyline outside.[542]

It is not until the final stanza that we get the speaker's 'I' and we are immediately brought into the world that the speaker is inhabiting. The opening line of the stanza, reminiscent once again of the 'The Hours of the Insomniac', also brings in a 'you':

> As I reach out, snatch at sleep
> sometimes it seems I catch your hand.[543]

There is a frailty in these lines; by the inclusion of the word 'sometimes' we are led to believe that the speaker is reaching out on an intermittent but regular basis, in between trying to sleep. The following lines, in a sentence over five lines, also offer elements of nature and the fusion of nature and the human:

> Or at the end, far along the breathless road
> you stand, arms full of flowers
> beside a wood in Normandy,
> mouth open with delight at the sight
> of the long green leaves, purple blossom.[544]

We have a possible double meaning with 'breathless road' which could refer to the journey that the speaker finds himself on, the breathlessness due to his medical condition or the stillness of a windless road. We also have the possibility that the speaker is not referring to memory here, but rather is experiencing a vision of sorts. More than likely it is the former. Henri was a frequent visitor to Normandy, to see his friend John Willett who had a house there in Le Thil. Henri's friendship with Willett stretched back to the 1960s, when Willett wrote and published 'Art in a City', about Liverpool's art scene.[545] It is safe to say that the 'you' of this poem is Catherine Marcangeli. After the strong visual image, one filled with happiness, the remainder of the stanza brings us back to the hospital. Again, it is unclear whether the image is clouded by lack of sleep, or is an actuality, partly by the reference to the song from Lewis Carroll's surreal *Alice's Adventures in Wonderland*:

> Along the gulping hours, moments torn,
> your face. Your voice, joining sleepy
> in The Lobster Quadrille. [...] [546]

The final line, a single sentence over three lines, is littered with meaning. If this is one of the last lines of poetry written by Adrian Henri, he managed to leave his readership with something special. He captures the essence of his poetics here, matched with his keen painterly eye. The yellow filament, reading his heartbeat on a screen, takes us back to that simplest of Henri motifs, the pink heart, used frequently in the 1960s.

During Henri's rehabilitation, plans continued for the 'Adrian Henri: Paintings 1953-1998' major retrospective at Liverpool's Walker Art Gallery. Henri had a long relationship with the gallery. Aside from being represented in several John Moores Prize exhibitions held at the Walker, he had, in 1977, curated an exhibition to celebrate the gallery's centenary, titled 'The Liverpool Academy Celebrates the Walker's 100th Birthday'. The Henri retrospective ran from 4 February until 2 April 2000.

Bel Mooney's feature on Henri from *The Times Magazine* allows us access to Henri's thoughts about his illness. He notes that he had changed because of it: 'Now I cry easily, it's just one recognition of the difference in me. [...] Now I can't take anything for granted; there is no get-out clause.'[547] In the article Marcangeli notes that Henri will be well enough to do a poetry gig the following year. She was right. Henri gave a reading at a special event in Liverpool, on 21 March 2000. Billed as 'A Celebration of Adrian Henri', the evening took place at Liverpool Philharmonic Hall, on Hope Street, a short distance from Henri's Mount Street home. During the spring of

2000 Liverpool was filled with banners advertising the Henri Walker retrospective, with Henri's trademark pink heart motif. Marcangeli recalls that 'it was quite nice for [Henri] to be wheeled down Hardman Street [in the city centre] seeing all those pink hearts lining the way.'[548] We can trace the love heart motif of Henri's back to his debut collection from 1968, *Tonight at Noon*. In the sequence, 'Poems Without Words', 'Love Poem IV' reads in its entirety:

A. Gives shockingpink hearts painted on squares of white
Paper to prettiest girls in audience.[549]

The pink heart also appears in the 1964 painting 'Liverpool 8 Four Seasons Painting'. The third of four panels in the work, representing Autumn, features the pink heart.[550] Henri had regained enough strength to sketch a small drawing for the flyer advertising the event. Recalling Henri's rehabilitation, Catherine Marcangeli remembers

He [Henri] got some movement back in his hand and became better at controlling it so he began drawing again – first just doodles as therapy – but then he began to improve. [...] he did a whole series of hospital flowers.[551]

Rather poignantly, the flyer sketch replicated the view that Henri had painted most recently with his 'The Day of the Dead, Hope Street' and 'Caleveras, Hope Street' paintings from 1998. In reference to The Beatles, Henri had handwritten on the sketch, in the form of a poster, 'For the benefit of Mr Henri, there will be a show tonight.'[552]

Writing on his website, musician and Henri collaborator Andy Roberts published an account of the Philharmonic event written by Paul Cary, who later would become webmaster for the Henri website. The event was indeed a celebration. The cast list was a Who's Who of Henri's friends and collaborators from his long career. The guests, who were introduced by Roger Philips of BBC Radio Merseyside, another friend of Henri's, included Brian Patten, Roger McGough, Henri's former girlfriend and future poet laureate Carol Ann Duffy, Mike McCartney, John Gorman, Willy Russell, Andy Roberts, George Melly and Tom Robinson. A personal highlight was the reformation of The Scaffold. It seemed not only fitting but highly appropriate to celebrate Henri with The Scaffold in attendance. Their brand of comedy and humour was well received and in keeping with the festive feeling of the event.

Henri made his last public reading, as Catherine Marcangeli had assured that he would, that night. Clearly frail, Henri managed to walk onto the stage, assisted by Catherine. His slow and thoughtful reading of a classic Henri poem, 'Love Is ... ' was extremely moving.

'Love Is ... ' is perhaps *the* typical Henri poem. Featured in *The Mersey Sound* and his debut collection *Tonight at Noon*, and opening *Selected and Unpublished*, the poem also appeared on the flyer for the 21 March 2000 celebration. The poem sits comfortably in its various books, however, it is interesting to note that the poem does not appear in *The Best of Henri: Selected Poems 1960-1970*, published by Jonathan Cape in 1975.

'Love Is ... ' relies on its rhythm, rhyme and repetition, motifs of the 'pop' poetry popularised during the 1960s by the publication of *The Mersey Sound*, the Edward Lucie-Smith edited anthology, *The Liverpool Scene, Pop Poetry, and Interviews Recorded Live along the Mersey Beat* and *Love, Love, Love: The New Love Poetry*, edited by Pete Roche.[553] It is a poem of its time, encapsulating the era in which it was written, and is among one of the most popular of Henri's poems. On the 40th Anniversary of *The Mersey Sound* tour undertaken by Patten and McGough, which featured an empty seat on-stage representing Henri, the poets would finish the reading by reciting, between them, 'Love Is ... '

The poem, five stanzas of four lines with the final line repeating the title, relies heavily on its song-like mode and repetition. The rhyme scheme in place thoughout the three of the four lines in each stanza is partially slanted in the first stanza:

Love is feeling cold in the back of vans
Love is a fanclub with only two fans
Love is walking paintstained hands
Love is [554]

The use of 'vans' and 'fans' brings to mind the Mersey Beat bands travelling in the wake of The Beatles and their fan club that clearly has more than two members. The reference to 'paintstained hands' (note the use of the compound word) is a clear nod to Henri's art practice.

The second stanza continues much in the same vein, but with a shift of emphasis towards the personal and relationships:

Love is fish and chips on Winter nights
Love is blankets full of strange delights
Love is when you don't put out the light
Love is [555]

The penultimate stanza continues the intimate tone of the second stanza with 'white panties lying all forlorn/Love is a pink nightdress still slightly warm/' and 'when you leave at dawn'.[556] There is a shift in the final stanza. The regular rhythm is dispensed with, though the rhyme scheme remains. Importantly, the final line carries the ellipsis of the poem's title allowing for the poem to fade, rather than end abruptly, while the only abbreviation of 'Love Is' to 'Love's' appears:

Love is you and love is me
Love is a prison and love is free
Love's what's there when you're away from me
Love is ... [557]

Henri's poor health continued throughout the year 2000. After the highs of the show at the Philharmonic in March, it must have been dispiriting for both Marcangeli and Henri to feel as though things were not getting any better. Henri suffered a further mini-stroke and was treated at Clatterbridge Hospital on the Wirral. Marcangeli had hoped, after learning of the reputation of a respected neuropsychologist, that the treatment would help with the various symptoms of the stroke.

Henri was well enough to attend a function at Liverpool City Council to learn that he was to be made a Freeman of the City. The day before he died it was announced that Roger McGough and Brian Patten were also to be made Freemen of the City. There's no doubt that Henri would have enjoyed the accolade bestowed upon him by the city. Joining such luminaries as Nelson Mandela, The Beatles and Bessie Braddock, the trade unionist and MP for Liverpool Exchange, Henri was in good company.[558]

Adrian Henri died at home in Mount Street on 21 December. His health had stabilized somewhat prior to his death. With the help of a nurse, Marcangeli and friends took turns to sit with him during his final hours.

Henri's funeral took place in Liverpool's Anglican Cathedral on 3 January 2001. The service, which was not religious, was a proper celebration of Henri the poet, artist and man. Mourners included McGough, Patten and Adrian Mitchell. Henri's former lovers, Carol Ann Duffy, Sue Sterne, Frances Hambidge and Heather Holden, were in attendance. The service sheet notes the contributions by Henri's brother Tony, Nell Dunn, Pete Morgan and Jackie Kay. The eulogy was given by Willy Russell and further contributions came from Adrian Mitchell, McGough and Patten.

The rear cover of the service sheet reproduces Henri's poem

'Evening Song' which was published in *City Hedges* in 1977, 1986's *Collected Poems*, and deemed important enough to feature in the 2007 *Selected and Unpublished*. The poem, reliant on its contrasts of night and day, is fittingly elegiac with 'Birds lie wrapped in nests of silence/I will come to you when the night is come' and the final stanza's matching 'Birds awake and sing the sunrise/I will love you till the day is come.'[559] After the internment at Toxteth Park Cemetery, rather fittingly, the wake took place at The Everyman on Hope Street. As Brian Patten noted, there was 'a huge crowd – a lot of people who were scattered around Adrian's life were there.'[560]

The funeral was a fitting send off for one of Liverpool's finest adopted sons. Henri was a brilliant advocate for the city, and in the aftermath of his passing, left a huge gap. He would, for certain, have relished Liverpool's status as European Capital of Culture in 2008, and perhaps also, relished the increase in tourism that the city has benefitted from since 2008. The UNESCO World Heritage status for the city's waterfront would have brought a smile to his face, with it being the location for his lines, 'Albion's most lovely daughter sat on the banks of the/Mersey dangling her landing stage in the water.'[561]

Notes

[434]Letter from Peter Robinson to Adrian Henri, dated 29 September 1995. The University of Liverpool, The Papers of Adrian Henri, Henri 3/2/36

[435]Adrian Henri, *Liverpool Accents: Seven Poets and a City*, p38.

[436]Adrian Henri, *Liverpool Accents: Seven Poets and a City*, p38.

[437]Ibid, p42. There is a double meaning by the inclusion of the word 'vague' in the poem. It means 'wave' in French.

[438]Ibid.

[439]Adrian Henri, 'Oyster' in *Liverpool Accents: Seven Poets and a City*, p43.

[440]Adrian Henri, 'Ballad of the Thames and Medway Barges' in *Liverpool Accents: Seven Poets and a City*, pp43-44.

[441]Ibid, p44.

[442]Adrian Henri, 'A City of Poems' in *Liverpool Accents: Seven Poets and a City*, p38.

[443]Letter from Tony Dash to Adrian Henri, The University of Liverpool, The Papers of Adrian Henri, Henri 3/2/42

[444]'Love in Blackpool' in *Liverpool Accents: Seven Poets and a City*, p38. The opening line is from the beginning of Stanley Holloway's 'Albert and the Lion', which Catherine Marcangeli remembers reciting for Henri: 'That's the beginning of Stanley Holloway's monologue, "Albert and the Lion", which I'd learnt by heart and used to recite for Adrian's amusement, attempting a Lancashire accent. It goes: "There's a famous seaside place called Blackpool/That's noted for fresh air and fun/Mr and Mrs Ramsbottom/Went there with young Albert their son".' Email from Catherine Marcangeli to the author, 18 November 2017.

[445]'Love in Blackpool' in *Liverpool Accents: Seven Poets and a City*, p38.

[446]'Love in Southport' in *Liverpool Accents: Seven Poets and a City*, p38.

[447]Ibid.

[448]Ibid.

[449]Carol Ann Duffy, rear cover of Catherine Marcangeli, ed, Adrian Henri, *Selected and Unpublished.*

[450]*Adrian Henri: Paintings 1953-1998.*

[451]Adrian Henri in *Adrian Henri: Paintings 1953-1998,* p128.

[452]Catherine Marcangeli points out that Henri would 'write on the canvas and then paint on top. Sometimes the paint would overlap, revealing parts of the writing, and sometimes the paint would cover the whole of the writing – so nobody except himself would know what was written underneath.' Email to the author, 18 November 2017.

[453]Adrian Henri in *Adrian Henri: Paintings 1953-1998,* p128.

[454]Adrian Henri in *Adrian Henri: Paintings 1953-1998,* p128.

[455]In an email to the author Marcangeli remembers the occasion and points out that she was 'sulking about something or other.' Email dated 18 November 2017.

[456]Adrian Henri in *Adrian Henri: Paintings 1953-1998,* p128.

[457]Ibid.

[458]Adrian Henri in *Adrian Henri: Paintings 1953-1998,* p128.

[459]Ibid.

[460]The painting appears in *Adrian Henri: Paintings 1953-1998,* p131 and the poem in *Adrian Henri: Selected and Unpublished,* ed. Catherine Marcangeli, pp144-146.

[461]'The Day of the Dead, Hope Street' in *Adrian Henri: Selected and Unpublished* Catherine Marcangeli, ed, pp144-146.

[462]Ibid.

[463]Ibid.

[464]It is worth noting that the cover of *Not Fade Away,* that features a detail of the painting, *The Entry of Christ Into Liverpool,* has airbrushed and removed the stencil lettering and the detail of the cat that Henri points

to in *Collected Poems*, p306.

[465]'The Day of the Dead, Hope Street' in *Adrian Henri: Selected and Unpublished*, Catherine Marcangeli, ed, pp144-147.

[466]Ibid, p144.

[467]'The Entry of Christ Into Liverpool' in *Adrian Henri: Selected and Unpublished*, Catherine Marcangeli, ed, p99.

[468]'The Day of the Dead, Hope Street' in *Adrian Henri: Selected and Unpublished*, Catherine Marcangeli, ed, p146.

[469]'The New, Fast, Automatic Daffodils' in *Adrian Henri: Selected and Unpublished*, Catherine Marcangeli, ed, p114.

[470]Ibid.

[471]'The New, Fast, Automatic Daffodils' in *Adrian Henri: Selected and Unpublished*, Catherine Marcangeli, ed, p114.

[472]Adrian Henri in *Adrian Henri: Selected and Unpublished*, Catherine Marcangeli, ed, p54.

[473]'Père Ubu in Liverpool' in. *Adrian Henri: Selected and Unpublished*, Catherine Marcangeli, ed, p209.

[474]'The New, Fast, Automatic Daffodils/Two' in *Adrian Henri: Selected and Unpublished*, Catherine Marcangeli, ed, p143.

[475]Email from Catherine Marcangeli to the author, 18 November 2017.

[476]'A Landscape for Adrian' in *Adrian Henri: Selected and Unpublished*, Catherine Marcangeli, ed, p243.

[477]Ibid.

[478]'Poem for Roger McGough' in *The Mersey Sound*, p42. See Chapter Four for more on this connection.

[479]'Cat Poem' in *The Mersey Sound*, p43.

[480]'Eco-Poem' in *Adrian Henri: Selected and Unpublished*, Catherine Marcangeli, ed, p243.

[481]These translations were undertaken as part of the Poetry International Festival in Rotterdam. Catherine Marcangeli remembers, 'Each year, a poet was chosen, and the poets taking part in the festival would hold translation workshops – eg basic translations of Breytenbach's original Afrikaans poems were provided into English, German and French. Then each of the poets would use those literal translation as a basis. The "chosen' poet was also present, and available to be asked questions. Then there was a reading where the poet would read his original, and then all the other poets would read their own translations. I took part in those workshops several times and it was really interesting.' Email to the author, 19 November 2017.

[482]Interview with Catherine Marcangeli and the author took place in Liverpool, 30 May 2005.

[483]www.lemonde.fr Accessed 14 May 2017.

[484]'What Were You Thinking About?' in *Adrian Henri: Selected and Unpublished*, Catherine Marcangeli, ed. p207.

[485]Ibid.

[486]'We Won't Forget That' in *Adrian Henri: Selected and Unpublished*, Catherine Marcangeli, ed, p246.

[487]For more about Bert Schierbeek and CoBrA, see the informative websites www.bertschierbeek.nl and www.huntfor.com/arthistory

[488]'We Won't Forget That' in *Adrian Henri: Selected and Unpublished*, Catherine Marcangeli, ed. p246.

[489]Catherine Marcangeli asked Willy Russell to read this poem as a conclusion to his speech at Henri's funeral in Liverpool. Email from Catherine Marcangeli to the author, 19 November 2017.

[490]'Mr Punch Speaks' in *Liverpool Accents: Seven Poets and a City*, p53.

[491]Catherine Marcangeli, email to the author, 19 November 2017.

[492]Peter Davies, *Arthur Ballard: Liverpool Artist and Teacher* (Abertillery: Old Bakehouse Publications, 1996), p9.

[493]An exhibition titled 'The Dinner Party: Of Time and Place' took place in

Birkenhead at the Williamson Art Gallery, and ran from 23 June – 3 September 2017. It reunited Adrian Henri, Arthur Ballard, Sam Walsh, Maurice Cockrill and Don McKinley. See the exhibition website for further details: www.thedinnerparty.space.

[494]Adrian Henri in Phil Bowen, *A Gallery to Play To*, p68.

[495]Ballard had told Henri in 1968 that he had to choose between being a teacher and being a rock 'n' roll star. The Liverpool Scene had been touring a lot at that time. Henri resigned. Catherine Marcangeli mentions that 'Adrian never held it against Arthur, as this enabled him to be a full-time artist, musician and poet. He was freelance from that time on, and thanked Arthur for that.' Email to the author, 19 November 2017. Racheal Eymond, Arthur Ballard's daughter, remembers the relationship between Ballard and Henri as being warm. She recalls visiting Henri with her father after Henri had had his heart attacks in 1970. Eymond recollects later walking along the promenade at Otterspool in Liverpool. The interview with Racheal Eymond took place in West Kirby, Wirral on 9 December 2017.

[496]'Mr Punch Speaks' in *Liverpool Accents: Seven Poets and a City*, p53.

[497]Ibid.

[498]'Mr Punch Speaks' in *Liverpool Accents: Seven Poets and a City*, p53.

[499]Ibid.

[500]Ibid.

[501]John Ashton, 'The Death of an Artist: Adrian Henri, 1932-2000' in *The Journal of Epidemiology and Community Healthcare,* Vol.56. pp. 72-75. http://www.jech.bmjjournals.com/ 6 April 2006. http://www.jech.bmjjournals.com/cgi/content/full/56/1/72#R7

[502]Adrian Henri, 'City 2000' uncollected poem, published in 'The Death of an Artist: Adrian Henri, 1932 – 2000' in *The Journal of Epidemiology and Community Healthcare,* Vol.56. pp. 72-75. http://www.jech.bmjjournals.com/ 6 April 2006. http://www.jech.bmjjournals.com/cgi/content/full/56/1/72#R7

[503]Charles Baudelaire, 'The Seven Old Men in' *The Complete Verse Volume I*, p177.

[504]Adrian Henri, 'A City of Poems' in *Liverpool Accents: Seven Poets and a City*, ed. Peter Robinson, p35. Regarding the title of the poem, Henri will have been aware of Roy Fisher's important text about Birmingham, 'City', first published in 1961and later collected in *The Dow Low Drop: New and Selected Poems* (Newcastle Upon Tyne: Bloodaxe, 1996). See also Robert Sheppard, *The Poetry of Saying: British Poetry and its Discontents 1950-2000*, pp77-81; and Peter Barry, *Contemporary British Poetry and the City* (Manchester: Manchester University Press, 2001), pp193-218.

[505]Adrian Henri, 'City 2000' uncollected poem, published in 'The Death of an Artist: Adrian Henri, 1932-2000'.

[506]See Ashton's article for a representation of the painting.

[507]Adrian Henri 'Ode to Dr Duncan' published in 'The Death of an Artist: Adrian Henri, 1932-2000'.

[508]Ibid.

[509]Ibid.

[510]Adrian Henri, from 'Notes on Painting and Poetry' in *Adrian Henri: Selected and Unpublished*, Catherine Marcangeli, ed, p247.

[511]The Bloodaxe Books website has no reference to Adrian Henri as one of the press's authors or any mention of the fact that *Not Fade Away* was published by the press.

[512]'The Image' in *Adrian Henri: Selected and Unpublished*, Catherine Marcangeli, ed, p286.

[513]Ibid.

[514]Ibid.

[515]Catherine Marcangeli remembers the poem being written in 2000: 'Adrian couldn't write by hand, so I'd got him a dictaphone. He dictated the poem, I typed it up, and he reworked it.' Email to the author, 19 November 2017.

[516]'The Image' in *Adrian Henri: Selected and Unpublished*, Catherine Marcangeli, ed, p286.

[517]'The Image' was a commission from Durham University for publication in their Alumni magazine.

[518]The poem is on the wall of an office at LJMU.

[519]'The Hours of the Insomniac' in *Adrian Henri: Selected and Unpublished*, Catherine Marcangeli, ed, p288.

[520]Ibid.

[521]'The Hours of the Insomniac' in *Adrian Henri: Selected and Unpublished*, Catherine Marcangeli, ed. p288.

[522]Ibid.

[523]'The Hours of the Insomniac' in *Adrian Henri: Selected and Unpublished*, Catherine Marcangeli, ed. p289.

[524]'The Hours of the Insomniac' in *Adrian Henri: Selected and Unpublished*, Catherine Marcangeli, ed, p289.

[525]Ibid.

[526]Ibid, p290.

[527]Ibid.

[528]'The Hours of the Insomniac' in *Adrian Henri: Selected and Unpublished*, Catherine Marcangeli, ed. p289.

[529]Ibid.

[530]Ibid, p291.

[531]'The Hours of the Insomniac' in *Adrian Henri: Selected and Unpublished*, Catherine Marcangeli, ed. p291.

[532]Ibid.

[533]Bel Mooney, 'Adrian Henri: Poet and Painter Extraordinary', *The Times Magazine*, 29 January 2000. Accessed at www.belmooney.co.uk < http://www.belmooney.co.uk/journalism/adrian_henri.html> April 13th 2017. This article, thankfully archived at Mooney's website, is a useful document, possibly Henri's last major interview. It contains photographs of Henri in Liverpool, at home in Mount Street and with

Catherine Marcangeli at his studio at the Bridewell Studios in Liverpool. Henri looks frail in the photographs. Mooney's descriptions of his recovery are rather touching.

[534]'Coronary Care Unit' in *Adrian Henri: Selected and Unpublished*, Catherine Marcangeli, ed, p81. The poem was first published in *Ambit* magazine #158 in 1999, with a poem written during the same period, 'Aubade, Ward "E"'.

[535]Ibid.

[536]Ibid.

[537]'Coronary Care Unit' in *Adrian Henri: Selected and Unpublished*, Catherine Marcangeli, ed. p81.

[538]Ibid.

[539]Ibid, p82.

[540]Ibid, p81.

[541]'Coronary Care Unit' in *Adrian Henri: Selected and Unpublished*, Catherine Marcangeli, ed. p81.

[542]Ibid, p82.

[543]'Coronary Care Unit' in *Adrian Henri: Selected and Unpublished*, Catherine Marcangeli, ed. p81.

[544]Ibid, p82.

[545]For more on Willett see the obituary by Richard Boston in the *Guardian* dated 22 August 2002 <https://www.theguardian.com/news/2002/aug/22/guardianobituaries.arts1> accessed 13 April 2017.

[546]'Coronary Care Unit' in *Adrian Henri: Selected and Unpublished*, Catherine Marcangeli, ed. p82.

[547]Bel Mooney, 'Adrian Henri: Poet and Painter Extraordinary', *The Times Magazine*, 29 January 2000.

[548]Catherine Marcangeli in Phil Bowen, *A Gallery to Play To*, p179. The pink heart motif is the first image to be seen on the Adrian Henri

website, www.adrianhenri.com, as the image is on the holding screen. It also appears on the front cover of *Collected Poems*. The back cover describes 'Cover design by Mick Keates incorporating a painting by Adrian Henri.' The painting, which is not represented in the *Adrian Henri: Paintings 1953-1998* exhibition catalogue, is a detail which features a handwritten 'Liverpool 8'. Consulting the Whitford Fine Art catalogue of the 'Pop & Protest: Adrian Henri Collage and Paintings from the Sixties' exhibition in March 1997, the painting is not included. There is a painting titled '24 Collages No 2 Hayley Mills Painting' which features a pink heart with 'Hayley' written in it. For those with a keen eye, the pink heart is also visible in his painting 'The Entry of Christ Into Liverpool'. It is located on the left-hand side of the painting next to the Campaign for Nuclear Disarmament (CND) flag.

[549]Adrian Henri, 'Love Poem IV' in *Tonight at Noon*, p29.

[550]Adrian Henri, 'Liverpool 8 Four Seasons Painting' in *Adrian Henri: Paintings 1953-1998*, p69.

[551]Catherine Marcangeli in Phil Bowen, *A Gallery to Play To*, p178.

[552]The flyer is available to view on the www.adrianhenri.com website, which is run by the Estate of Adrian Henri. The Beatles reference stems from the opening lines of the song 'Being for the Benefit of Mr Kite'. The song appeared on The Beatles' 1967 album 'Sgt Pepper's Lonely Hearts Club Band'. It is no coincidence that this was the year that *The Mersey Sound* was published by Penguin Books.

[553]See Pete Roche, ed, *Love, Love, Love: The New Love Poetry* (London: Corgi Books, 1967).

[554]'Love Is ... ' in Adrian Henri, *Tonight at Noon*, p45.

[555]Ibid.

[556]'Love Is ... ' in Adrian Henri, *Tonight at Noon*, p45.

[557]Ibid.

[558]Catherine Marcangeli recalls Henri's reaction to the news: 'When it was announced, at that function, Adrian explained to me that it was a big deal, especially as Bob Paisley was also a Freeman of the City.' (Paisley is Liverpool FC's most successful manager.) Email to the author, 19

November 2017.

[559]'Evening Song' in Adrian Henri, *Collected Poems*, p199.

[560]Brian Patten in Phil Bowen, *A Gallery to Play To*, p181. I was in attendance at the service at the Cathedral. Patten is right, there was a huge congregation and a lot of members of the public were in attendance to pay their respects. The great West Door of the Cathedral, only opened during special circumstances, such as the visit of Pope John Paul II in 1982, was in use the day of the funeral.

[561]'Mrs Albion, You've Got a Lovely Daughter' in *The Mersey Sound*, p5.

6

LEGACY

Poet, painter, pataphysician, I was in awe of Adrian when I first met
him in the mid-1960s. He was able to select and use the best of the
tsunami of bewildering new ideas and art forms breaking over our
shores. He helped change Britain for the better.

— Barry Miles[562]

ADRIAN HENRI'S LEGACY CONTINUES TO GROW since his
death. The tireless work of Catherine Marcangeli in promoting his
work has been instrumental in this. Henri's art continues to grace
gallery walls across the UK. In 2015 a major event took place at
London's Institute of Contemporary Arts. 'First Happenings: Adrian
Henri in the '60s and '70s' built on an exhibition during the 2014
Liverpool Biennial, called 'Total Art: Adrian Henri', at Liverpool
John Moores University from 5 July-25 November.

The Liverpool exhibition coincided with a new publication edited
by Marcangeli, *Adrian Henri: Total Artist*. Though concentrating
on Henri's instigation and involvement in the Happenings in
Liverpool in the early 1960s, alongside his musical career and wider
art practice, room is made for a short selection of poetry, titled 'In

the Top 20: Selected Poems'. The six poems included are: 'Tonight at Noon', 'I Want to Paint', 'Mrs Albion, You've Got a Lovely Daughter', 'Love Is ... ', 'Me', and 'Batpoem'.

The ICA exhibition featured a special panel event to consider 'and re-evaluate Henri's work and his broader significance beyond the labels of "Liverpool poet" and "Pop painter".'[563] Panellists included Catherine Marcangeli and Barry Miles and it was chaired by Liverpool's Bluecoat artistic director, Brian Biggs. It is pleasing to see that Henri's work is being recognised in such august institutions as the ICA and Liverpool Art School (LJMU).[564]

In terms of the poetry Henri's profile was temporarily raised by the *Selected and Unpublished* in 2007, alongside the 40th Anniversary reissue of *The Mersey Sound* as a Penguin Modern Classic. In October 2007 ITV's culture and arts programme, The South Bank Show, featured McGough and Patten discussing the book, in the old Everyman Theatre on Hope Street, while Henri made an appearance via archive footage.

Henri further made his presence felt in *Writing Liverpool*, published in 2007 by Liverpool University Press, and edited by Michael Murphy and Deryn Rees-Jones. His 1968 painting, 'Père Ubu in Liverpool', graces the cover. The image, an updated version of the 1962 painting of the same name, features Ubu with his trademark black umbrella among a series of images, locating him in Liverpool landmarks such as the Metropolitan Cathedral of Christ the King and the Liver Building.[565]

Henri and his work also feature on The Poetry Archive website. This site, founded by Andrew Motion when he was poet laureate, presents audio recordings of poets reading their work, alongside biographical details. Henri's selection features 'Death in the Suburbs', which the site notes as coming from *Collected Poems*. Whilst this is true, the poem actually opens 1980's book, *From the*

Loveless Motel. At first it may seem a strange choice as it is not one of the more famous 1960s poems. Henri writes about the poem on the site and describes his process.[566]

In 2016 Carol Ann Duffy, alongside then National Poet of Wales Gillian Clarke, edited an anthology published by Faber and Faber, called *The Map and the Clock: A Laureate's Choice of the Poetry of Britain and Ireland.* In this wide-ranging anthology covering the past 1400 years, Henri is featured in the section titled 'Hi Yih, Yippety-yap, Merrily I Flow ... ' which covers the post-war years of 1945-1970. Also featuring in this section are the likes of Dylan Thomas, Sylvia Plath, Rosemary Tonks, Basil Bunting and Henri's old friend, Adrian Mitchell. The featured Henri poem is 'Tonight at Noon'.[567]

We must remember that Henri was an established children's poet, alongside McGough and Patten, who both write for children. It is interesting to note that Henri chose not to illustrate his children's poetry collections. The children's poetry market is a strong one. School libraries stock books and visiting schools is a valuable source of income for writers and a chance to sell books. Henri was no different to other working writers and regularly visited schools to perform his children's poetry. What is unusual is that Henri made use of his adult poetry in certain volumes of his children's verse and employed techniques that he used throughout his writing career. In 1987's *The Phantom Lollipop Lady and Other Poems* a poem titled 'A Poem for my Cat' appears. To older readers familiar with Henri's work, the poem would be recognisable as 'Cat Poem', which featured in major Henri publications.[568]

Similarly, Henri's interest in Haiku transferred from the adult collections to the children's verse. Often following the prescribed syllabic count, he would, at times, veer from this and the traditional subject matter of the form:

Haiku: City Park in Winter
Snowdrops stand up stiff
twilight nurses
round the darkening flowerbeds.[569]

and 'NoHaiku' follows, with deliberate irony, the traditional form,
aside from its subject matter:

I'm sorry to say
that I really don't feel like
a haiku today.[570]

An interesting example of a mix of Henri's capability of writing
haiku for children is evidenced in *Robocat*. In a seasonal sequence,
titled 'Four Seasons Haiku', we are reminded of the 1975 privately-
published *Haiku*, later gathered in the *Collected Poems*:

1
Yellow rapefields glow;
hedges dipped in mayblossom:
cream in a green bowl.

2
flags hang limp from masts;
buddleias flop exhausted
on August pavements.

3
folding up fruit-nets;
already a trawl of leaves
in their green meshes.

4
take away one word:
a tall chimney collapses
in the winter wood.[571]

Here we see that Henri resorts to the compound words of his early career and ensures that the images are straightforward, taking into account his intended audience. Similarly, Henri's children's poetry continues the themes that were prevalent in the adult poetry. These crossover themes include politics: *Robocat* contains a poem titled 'Refugee' and *Dinner With The Spratts* contains 'Song of the Earth (for Environment Week, Merseyside, 1990) which mixes those familiar Henri themes of nature and the urban: 'Curled tendrils of fern/peer hopefully through bin-bags, chip-papers,/choke on polystyrene. Green water fights for its breath amid the stink of sewage,/black rainbows of oil.' The poem continues with arguably the most important environmental message, the impact of the human on the landscape: 'Our leavings mark/their riverside.'[572]

As if to counter the possibly difficult enjambment for younger readers, Henri offers a tight couplet, italicised for emphasis, designed as a call to action, to finish the opening stanza of the poem:

> *So bring your wellies, bring your macs,*
> *never mind sore feet or aching backs.*[573]

Henri continued the ecocritical theme with a local lens making reference to the set of three tidal islands off the coast of the Wirral on Merseyside: 'Take a dawn walk on Hilbre. Wait/in the silvery light to see the birds migrate'.[574] The repeated coda, in the form of rhyming couplets reinforces the poem's message:

> *So bring your raincoats, bring your boots,*
> dig in the earth and find your roots.
>
> *Life is short but the earth is long*
> *put your ear to the ground and hear its song.*[575]

There is a rather poignant poem in 1993's *Dinner with the Spratts* that foreshadows Henri's final poem, 'Coronary Care Unit'. The poem, 'Children's Ward', is narrated from the perspective of a child awaiting the visit from her/his mother: 'I wonder if she'll be/as glad to see me?/Twenty-five minutes./I wonder what's for tea?'[576]

There seem, at times, to be interesting crossovers with Henri's adult poetry and the work for children. He titles a poem after his 1977 collection, *City Hedges*, and uses the cut-up technique highlighted by the construction of 'The New, Fast, Automatic Daffodils' in one of his children's poems, 'Night Comics'.[577] The poem acknowledges the technique and its source material as being 'cut-up from one issue of *The Beano*'. The poem, dedicated to the cultural activist, producer and writer and former director of the ICA, Michael Kustow, feels like a genuine cut-up. If we look at the opening four lines of the twenty-line single-stanza poem, we can see its randomness:

> Hee-hee. I should get plenty of presents in this!
> I got sneezing powder A A A A CHOO!
> ERK. I'm locked in!
> CRUMBS. If only I hadn't crocked my ankle! [578]

The use of exclamation marks and lexis designed for comic readers of a young age, lends weight to the fact that Henri used a faithful cut-up technique to construct the poem.

***

2017 saw celebrations in Liverpool for the fiftieth anniversary of the publication of *The Mersey Sound*. Today Liverpool is a very different place to what it was when the book was first published. There is a willingness to celebrate the cultural impact that the city has had on national and, indeed, global culture. It is difficult to imagine the city today ordering the destruction of an important music venue such as The Cavern; there is a greater understanding of the need to preserve its cultural heritage. Partly this new awareness can be traced back to Liverpool's year of being European Capital of Culture in 2008, but also the managed decline of the city from various Conservative governments.

To celebrate this anniversary, a series of events took place in the city. The celebrations, titled 'Tonight at Noon' after the Henri poem (and the Charles Mingus album that Henri took the title from), began on the 12 April, and were part of a wider city-wide celebration, '67-17: 50 Summers of Love'. Other events in the '50 Summers of Love' included a performance of French musique concrete composer Pierre Henry's *Messe de Liverpool*, a mass that was originally commissioned for the opening of Liverpool's Metropolitan Cathedral of Christ the King in 1967. Roger McGough returned to the stage of the Liverpool Philharmonic Hall for two performances of his poem *Summer with Monika*, again to celebrate the fiftieth anniversary of its original publication.

Of course celebrations were also plentiful for the fiftieth anniversary of the release of The Beatles' seminal album, *Sgt Pepper's Lonely Hearts Club Band*, originally released on 26 May 1967. Internationally acclaimed artists such as Judy Chicago were commissioned by Tate Liverpool to respond to songs from the album. Roger McGough narrated a performance of the album by Beatles tribute band, The Bootleg Beatles.

The Mersey Sound's publication date in 1967 was 25 May. A series of events took place on the day of the anniversary, including recordings of the three poets reading from *The Mersey Sound* being played on the Mersey Ferries during the commuter run. Local universities, Liverpool John Moores and Edge Hill, played recordings throughout the day on their respective campuses. A reading to celebrate the day took place at the Everyman Theatre, organised by Edge Hill University students, with special surprise visitor, Roger McGough.

Adrian Henri loomed large in the celebrations. An exhibition curated by Catherine Marcangeli took place for the duration of the 'Tonight at Noon' celebrations, at the city's neo-classical St Georges's Hall. The exhibition, entitled 'Adrian Henri: Poet/Painter/ Performer', was noteworthy for the foregrounding of his poetic practice. Set in a corridor under the main hall (where once prisoners awaited in cells before their appearance in the courts above), it highlighted the best of Henri. A print of 'The Entry of Christ Into Liverpool' sat alongside a poster-poem of the work. Its caption read:

> In this homage to James Ensor's 'Entry of Christ Into Brussels in 1889', Henri relocated the scene to Liverpool. A few years before the Sgt Pepper album cover, he gathered a cast of heroes (Charlie Mingus, Père Ubu ...) and friends (poets Brian Patten, Pete Brown, Roger McGough, writer George Melly, photographer Philip Jones-Griffiths and The Beatles ...)[579]

A more general exhibition, 'The Mersey Sound Archives', took place at Liverpool Central Library in the grand space of the Hornby Library. Again, expertly curated by Catherine Marcangeli, using material from the Adrian Henri Estate and the University of Liverpool's Liverpool Poets Collections, the exhibition gathered ephemera and original handwritten notices by Henri advertising Happenings, such as a 'Night' at Sampson and Barlow's featuring Henri, McGough and Patten, alongside original promotional posters for books such as *Love, Love, Love: The New Love Poetry*, which featured among others, Henri, McGough and Patten.[580]

Further events under the 'Tonight at Noon' banner, included a performance by The Thurston Moore Group at St George's Hall, during which Moore recited a poem by each of the poets featured in *The Mersey Sound.* Five award-winning poets were commissioned to respond to *The Mersey Sound* and perform alongside McGough and Patten.[581] A more Henri oriented event, 'Horny Handed Tons of Soil', took place at the Unity Theatre in Liverpool, to finish off the 'Tonight at Noon' celebrations.[582]

It is clear that *The Mersey Sound* has had a major cultural impact since its publication. Penguin Books marked the occasion of its Fiftieth Anniversary with another reissue. This time the 'restored' edition featured a Henri painting, 1961's *Small Fairground Image 3* and restored the contents to those of the original edition from 1967.[583]

Henri's poetry can be seen as being both populist and cutting edge. The reader can trace this back through work like the aforementioned 'Tonight at Noon' and perhaps more noticeably with poems such as 'The Entry of Christ Into Liverpool' with its companion painting and poster and their engagement with the avant-garde poetics.

From the beginnings of the Happenings in Liverpool on Hope Street in 1962 to gracing the stage on the Philharmonic Hall on the same street in 2000, Adrian Henri has left a huge mark on the city of Liverpool. His poetry and its influence is wide ranging and as the celebratory events in Liverpool in 2017 showed, Henri is remembered with fondness for the massive role he played in the cultural life of the city. Beyond the city, with major exhibitions, that showcase both his art and poetry, Henri is remembered as both an innovator and facilitator, whose love for the various modes of art left a legacy that should endure and inspire future generations of poets and artists.

Notes

[562]*Adrian Henri: Total Artist*. The quote by Miles appears on the rear cover.

[563]The ICA website features a video of the panel discussion. See www.ica.art <accessed 23 May 2017>

[564]For a full list of Henri exhibitions, see the Henri website, www.adrianhenri.com

[565]Michael Murphy and Deryn Rees-Jones, eds, *Writing Liverpool: Essays and Interviews* (Liverpool: Liverpool University Press, 2007). For more on Ubu and Henri's relationship with him, see p15.

[566]See the Poetry Archive site http://www.poetryarchive.org/poem/death-suburbs <accessed 23 May 2017>

[567]Carol Ann Duffy and Gillian Clarke, eds. *The Map and the Clock: A Laureate's Choice of the Poetry of Britain and Ireland*, (London: Faber and Faber, 2016).

[568]'A Poem for my Cat' in *The Phantom Lollipop Lady and Other Poems* (London: Methuen Children's Books, 1987), p21. It is worth noting that the poem appeared in the 1983 revised edition of *The Mersey Sound* as part of the 'Short Poems' section, but was omitted from the original 1967 edition, and, as a consequence, the 2017 restored edition. The poem was included in Henri's 1986 *Collected Poems*. Catherine Marcangeli thought the poem significant enough to feature in the posthumous collection, *Selected and Unpublished*.

[569]'Haiku: City Park in Winter' in *The World's Your Lobster* (London: Bloomsbury Children's Books, 1998), p48.

[570]'NoHaiku' in *Robocat* (London: Bloomsbury Children's Books, 1998), p34.

[571]'Four Seasons Haiku' in *Robocat*, p54.

[572]'Song of the Earth' in *Dinner With The Spratts* (London: Methuen Children's Books, 1993), p50.

[573]Ibid.

[574]Ibid, p53.

[575]Ibid.

[576]'Children's Ward' in *Dinner With The Spratts*, p42.

[577]For more about 'The New, Fast, Automatic Daffodils' and the cut-up technique adopted by Henri, see Chapter 5, p127. 'Night Comics' in Adrian Henri, *The Phantom Lollipop Lady and Other Poems*.

[578]'Night Comics' in Adrian Henri, *The Phantom Lollipop Lady and Other Poems*, p58.

[579]The author visited the exhibition on 13 May 2017. The accompanying promotional flyer for the 'Tonight at Noon' events with Henri's trademark pink love heart prominent on it, describes the exhibition thus: Adrian Henri was a 'total artist' – he came to prominence as a poet in 1967 alongside Roger McGough and Brian Patten, but he had trained as a painter, set up the first Happenings in Britain, and exhibited widely. Dubbed by John Peel 'one of the great non-singers of our time', Henri also fronted the unlikely poetry-and-rock band Liverpool Scene. In 1969 they supported Led Zeppelin, played the Isle of Wight Festival and toured America. In this exhibition, 1960s artworks, poems and original rock posters offer a glimpse of Henri's multi-faceted talents.

[580]The author visited this exhibition on 13 May 2017. The accompanying promotional flier for the 'Tonight at Noon' events, describes the exhibition thus: In 1967, *The Mersey Sound* brought poetry down from the shelf and onto the street, capturing the mood of the Sixties. A publishing phenomenon, it went on to become the bestselling poetry anthology of all time. Whether they wrote of young love, pop idols, atomic bombs, eccentric bus conductors or sci-fi superheroes, the Liverpool Poets were contemporary, urban and accessible. Through their books and live readings, they made poetry a part of popular culture. This exhibition, curated by Catherine Marcangeli, unearths a display of original manuscripts, ephemera, posters, audio and video material – all of which retraces the emergence of Adrian Henri, Roger McGough and Brian Patten onto the 1960s poetry scene.

[581]The reading at Liverpool's Bluecoat Arts Centre featured Paul Farley, Deryn Rees-Jones, Lizzie Nunnery, Eleanor Rees and Andrew McMillan.

[582]According to the Unity Theatre website, 'Horny Handed Tons of Soil' is inspired by Henri's poetic response to the urban geography of Liverpool and will explore the themes of destruction, construction and memory within the stories of what has been lost and found, in the re-sculpting of the Liverpool landscape over the last fifty years. < https://www.unitytheatreliverpool.co.uk/whats-on/hornyhanded-tons-of-soil.html> accessed 30 June 2017.

[583]See the appendix for the various running orders for the various editions.

BIBLIOGRAPHY

Ashton, John, 'The Death of an Artist: Adrian Henri, 1932-2000' in *The Journal of Epidemiology and Community Healthcare*, Vol 56, pp72-75. Accessed online http://jech.bmjjournals.com/cgi/content/full/56/1/72#R7

Barry, Peter, *Contemporary British Poetry and the City* (Manchester: Manchester University Press, 2000).

Baudelaire, Charles, *The Complete Verse*, trans. Francis Scarfe (London: Anvil Poetry Press, 1986).

Baudelaire, Charles, *The Poems in Prose*, trans. Francis Scarfe (London: Anvil Poetry Press, 1989).

Belcham, John, *Merseypride: Essays in Liverpool Exceptionalism* (Liverpool: Liverpool University Press, 2006).

Bowen, Phil, *A Gallery to Play To: The Story of the Mersey Poets* (Liverpool: Liverpool University Press, 2007).

Bukowski, Charles, *Slouching Toward Nirvana* (New York: Ecco/Harper Collins, 2005).

Burroughs, William S., *A William Burroughs Reader* (London: Picador, 1982).

Cookson, Linda, *Brian Patten: Writers and their Work* (Plymouth: Northcote Hall, 1997).

Du Noyer, Paul, *Liverpool: Wondrous Place* (London: Virgin Books, 2002).

Grunenberg, Christoph and Knifton, Robert eds, *Centre of the Creative Universe: Liverpool and the Avant-Garde* (Liverpool: Liverpool University Press, 2007).

Davies, Peter, *Arthur Ballard: Liverpool Artist and Teacher* (Abertillery: Old Bakehouse Productions, 1996).

Duffy, Carol Ann and Clarke, Gillian, eds, *The Map and the Clock: A Laureate's Choice of the Poetry of Britain and Ireland* (London: Faber and Faber, 2016).

Eliot, T.S., *Collected Poems* (London: Faber and Faber, 2015).

Gray, Richard, *Francophone African Poetry and Drama: A Cultural History since the 1960s* (North Carolina: McFarland and Company, 2014).

Hampson, Robert, *Seaport* (Exeter: Shearsman Books, 2008).

Henri, Adrian, *Tonight at Noon* (London: Rapp and Whiting, 1968).

Henri, Adrian, *City* (London: Rapp and Whiting, 1968).

Henri, Adrian, *Autobiography* (London: Jonathan Cape, 1971).

Henri, Adrian, *America* (London: Turret Books, 1972).

Henri, Adrian, *Total Art: Environments, Happenings and Performance* (New York: Praeger, 1974).

Henri, Adrian, *The Best of Henri* (London: Jonathan Cape, 1975).

Henri, Adrian, *Penny Arcade* (London: Jonathan Cape, 1983).

Henri, Adrian, *Collected Poems 1967-85* (London: Allison and Busby, 1986).

Henri, Adrian, *The Phantom Lollipop Lady and Other Poems* (London: Magnet Children's Books, 1987).

Henri, Adrian, *Wish You Were Here* (London: Jonathan Cape, 1990).

Henri, Adrian, *Dinner With The Spratts* (London: Methuen Children's Books, 1993).

Henri, Adrian, *Not Fade Away* (Newcastle upon Tyne: Bloodaxe, 1994).

Henri, Adrian, *Art of the Sixties* (London: Whitford Fine Art, 1997).

Henri, Adrian, *Robocat* (London: Bloomsbury Children's Books, 1998).

Henri, Adrian, *The World's Your Lobster: The Very Best Collected Poems* (London: Bloomsbury Children's Books, 1998).

Henri, Adrian, *Adrian Henri: Paintings 1953-1998* (Liverpool: National Museums and Galleries on Merseyside, 2000).

Henri, Adrian, *Spooky Poems* (London: Bloomsbury Children's Books, 2001).

Henri, Adrian, *Selected and Unpublished Poems 1965-2000*, ed, Catherine Marcangeli (Liverpool: Liverpool University Press, 2007).

Henri, Adrian; McGough, Roger and Patten, Brian, *New Volume* (London: Penguin, 1983).

Henri, Adrian; McGough, Roger and Patten, Brian, *The Mersey Sound* (London: Penguin, 1988).

Higgins, D.S., *Wider Aspects of English* (London: Cassell, 1974).

Housman, A.E., *A Shropshire Lad and Other Poems* (London, Penguin Classics, 2010).

Landry, Charles, *The Creative City* (London: Earthscan, 2000).

Lucas, Martin, *Stepping Stones: A Way into Haiku* (Ramsgate: The British Haiku Society, 2007).

Lucie-Smith, Edward, *The Liverpool Scene* (New York: Doubleday, 1968).

Marcangeli, Catherine, ed. *Adrian Henri: Total Artist* (London: Occasional Papers, 2014).

McGough, Roger, *Watchwords* (London: Jonathan Cape, 1969).

McGough, Roger, *Melting Into the Foreground* (London: Penguin, 1987).

McGough, Roger, *Selected Poems 1967-1987* (London: Jonathan Cape, 1989).

McGough, Roger, *Said and Done: The Autobiography* (London: Century, 1997).

Murphy, Michael and Rees-Jones, Deryn, *Writing Liverpool* (Liverpool: Liverpool University Press, 2007).

Miles, Barry, *In the Sixties* (London: Pimlico, 2003).

Miles, Barry, *London Calling: A Countercultural History of London Since 1945* (London: Atlantic, 2010).

Patten, Brian, *Little Johnny's Confession* (London: George Allen and Unwin, 1971).

Patten, Brian, *Love Poems* (London: Flamingo, 1992).

Patten, Brian, *Storm Damage* (London: Flamingo, 1995).

Patten, Brian, *Armada* (London: Flamingo, 1996).

Roche, Pete, ed. *Love, Love, Love: The New Love Poetry* (London: Corgi, 1967).

Robinson, Peter, ed. *Liverpool Accents: Seven Poets and a City* (Liverpool: Liverpool University Press, 1996).

Sheppard, Robert, *The Poetry of Saying: British Poetry and its Discontents 1950-2000* (Liverpool: Liverpool University Press, 2004).

Tester, Keith, ed. *The Flâneur* (London: Routledge 1994).

Wade, Stephen, ed, *Gladsongs and Gatherings: Poetry and its Social Context in Liverpool since the 1960s* (Liverpool: Liverpool University Press, 2001).

Warren-Smith, Gabriella and Simpson, Colin David, *The Dinner Party: Of Time and Place* (Liverpool and Birkenhead: Hope University and Williamson Art Gallery and Museum, 2017).

Walsh, Sam, *Sam Walsh* (Liverpool: National Museums and Galleries on Merseyside, 1991).

Willett, John, *Art in a City* (Liverpool: Liverpool University Press, 2007).

Williams, Williams Carlos, *Selected Essays of William Carlos Williams* (New York, New Directions, 1969).

APPENDIX

Adrian Henri poems and running order, contained in the various editions of *The Mersey Sound.*

Penguin Modern Poets 10: *The Mersey Sound* edition,
(Harmondsworth: Penguin, 1967)

Tonight at Noon

Adrian Henri's Last Will and Testament

Liverpool Poems

Without You

Love Is ...

Morning Poem

Drinking Song

Song for a Beautiful Girl Petrol-pump Attendant on the Motorway

Poem for Roger McGough

Song of Affluence *or* I Wouldn't Leave My 8-Roomed House for You

Love Poem/Colour Supplement

On the Late Late Massachers Stillbirths and Deformed Children a Smoother Lovelier Skin Job

Great War Poems

Country Song

Holcombe Poem/Poem For a Girl I Didn't Meet

Me

Hello Adrian

Adrian Henri's Talking After Christmas Blues

The Blazing Hat, Part Two

Pictures From an Exhibition

Love Poem

Wild West Poems

Poem in Memoriam T.S. Eliot

Where'er You Walk

The New 'Our Times'

In the Midnight Hour

I Want To Paint

Don't Worry/Everything's Going to be All Right

Mrs Albion, You've Got a Lovely Daughter

New Volume (Harmondsworth: Penguin, 1983)

Death in the Suburbs

Hostage

Citysong

Autumn Leaving

from 'Autobiography'

Metropolis

A Song for A.E. Housman

Don't Look

Butterfly

Epilogue

Poem for Liverpool 8

Scenes from the Permissive Society

Spring Poem

The Triumph of Death

Two Lullabys

An Incident at Longueville

Girl Bathing

Words Without a Story

Red Card

A Song in April

The Dance of Death

Short Poems

Night Carnation

Any Prince to Any Princess

Morning Song

The Mersey Sound: Revised edition (London: Penguin, 1983)

Tonight at Noon

Mrs Albion, You've Got a Lovely Daughter

Adrian Henri's Talking After Christmas Blues

In the Midnight Hour

Love Is ...

The New 'Our Times'

I Want To Paint

Adrian Henri's Last Will and Testament

Without You

Liverpool Poems

Nightsong

Bomb Commercials

Who?

Batpoem

Galactic Lovepoem

Love From Arthur Rainbow

Me

The Entry of Christ Into Liverpool

The New, Fast, Automatic Daffodils

See The Conkering Heroine Comes

Short Poems

from 'City', Part Three

Car Crash Blues

Spring Song for Mary

The Mersey Sound: Modern Classics edition (London: Penguin, 2007)

Tonight at Noon

Mrs Albion, You've Got a Lovely Daughter

Adrian Henri's Talking After Christmas Blues

In the Midnight Hour

Love Is ...

The New 'Our Times'

I Want To Paint

Adrian Henri's Last Will and Testament

Without You

Liverpool Poems

Nightsong

Bomb Commercials

Who?

Batpoem

Galactic Lovepoem

Love From Arthur Rainbow

Me

The Entry of Christ Into Liverpool

The New, Fast, Automatic Daffodils

See The Conkering Heroine Comes

Poem in Memoriam T.S. Eliot

Where'er You Walk

Car Crash Blues

Spring Song for Mary

The Mersey Sound: Restored 50th Anniversary Edition (London: Penguin, 2017)

Tonight at Noon

Adrian Henri's Last Will and Testament

Index